I'm Not a
CRAZY CABBIE

A Memoir of a Chicago Cabdriver

Chuck Okofor

iUniverse LLC
Bloomington

I'M NOT A CRAZY CABBIE
A MEMOIR OF A CHICAGO CABDRIVER

iUniverse books may be ordered through booksellers or by contacting:

iUniverse LLC
1663 Liberty Drive
Bloomington, IN 47403
www.iuniverse.com
1-800-Authors (1-800-288-4677)

ISBN: 978-1-4917-3569-5 (sc)
ISBN: 978-1-4917-3568-8 (e)

Library of Congress Control Number: 2014909864

Printed in the United States of America.

iUniverse rev. date: 06/03/2014

Chapter 1

ROOKIE CABBIE GOES TO WORK

The temperature was some degrees below zero and the ground still white with some inches of frozen snow that had fallen the previous days. It was on this very cold Chicago wintery and windy morning of January, 1996 that I chose to make my debut as a cabbie.

I had dressed very warmly with several layers of clothes to beat the notorious Chicago wind chill factor of the cold. I boarded the Metra train from my South suburb residence to Chicago..The ride with Metra was so warm and comfortable that I wished I had chosen a different day than today to begin work.

I disembarked from the train at Roosevelt after missing the 18th street train stop. 18th street would have been the nearest stop for me to get to Yellow Cab Company office at 18th and Indiana, but since I missed to drop off at 18th, I had to take the punishment from the bitter and piercing cold weather by walking to Yellow Cab office. The walk from Roosevelt to 18th and Indiana, a distance of about half a mile was very long and tortuous. The chilly wind on my bare face caused some partial loss of feeling on my face. My nose was running and steady tears in my eyes inhibited my sight. Even though I had a thick sock in my boots, I was beginning to lose feeling in my toes. At one point I thought of hailing a cab to take me the rest of the way, but I was able to muster enough courage to finish the trek.

I arrived at the Yellow Cab cashier front desk and waiting area at about 6.15 am and went straight to the restroom to clean up. My face was kind of puffed up and my eyes and nose red due to constant cleaning of the tears and the running nose..My mustache was caked with whitish and sticky substance I realized was the unclean remnants of the partly frozen and partly dried mucus from my nose.

"' Next in line!', the cashier called out from behind the bulletproof protected glass counter. I glanced around and found all the eyes of men I presumed were cab drivers who had come to lease cabs, were on me.

I got up with a start and casually said : 'Its me' as I stepped forward to the counter. The cashier slapped a car key with a number tag on it on the counter. I stood there with my right palm covering the key waiting for further instructions.

"' Next in line please', the cashier announced again. Then I sensed that he must be thinking he has done with me. With a puzzled look on my face I said to him:"'sir, this is my first day, what do I do next"

"Uh, you're a rookie?" he asked, with a chuckle under his breath.

"Yes", I replied.

Then he took time to explain the procedures to me. First of all I need to go out to the parking lot and search for the cab whose number is on the key. Check it out ; test drive it and check for any problem with the drive or damage on the body like dents or scratches.

If I am satisfied with the condition of the car then to come back and complete the payment procedures and then I am ready to go make money.

I picked up the cab from among tens of other Yellow cabs parked in the parking lot. It was a worn and beaten Chevy Caprice which runs well though. I completed all the paper work around 7.25 am ; filled up my tank and drove my cab straight to the Hyatt Regency Hotel on east Wacker Drive. I queued up at the hotel cab stand on Wacker and Stetson. The cab line was full, but moving steadily and without long wait I was the next to pick up. My heart has begun to beat faster and I have begun wondering where the destination of my very first fare would be. Would he be going to a familiar address within downtown or somewhere outside downtown that might pose a problem to me? Then the whistle sounded: that was the signal from the doorman to the next cab in the line to pull up for a pickup. Now I could almost hear the pounding of my heart in my chest. My palms have begun to sweat as one man who from his look may have come from Asia; possibly from Japan, stepped up and boarded my cab and announced:' 'McCormick Place North''.

I breathed a breath of relief.. McCormick Place East, South and North are easy ones to go to, I thought. After all, l I had made practice runs to them during my personal practice drives around downtown Chicago. I drove out, turned right and headed to the South Lake Shore Drive. That was a much more direct route to McCormick Place North. Then I turned to my passenger after I had stolen a look at him from my rear view mirror, and asked with a professional voice: 'How's your day going?'

'Very cold ; Chicago very very cold,' he replied in his smattering English.

'Yeah' Chicago is very cold 'I agreed. I recalled reading some information on the bill board of Yellow Cab cashier office about the international convention beginning that day at the McCormick Place north.

'So where are you coming from?'

'South Korea'

'Oh, South Korea; you're welcome. How do you like the city?'

'Chicago, very beautiful.'

The traffic on the south bound Lake Shore Drive was relatively light so vehicles were moving steadily on about 35 mph. I sighted the Field Museum and then the Soldier Field. These are my land marks. I am close now, I thought ----- there you go! I could see my destination about half mile away. I was excited that in a few minutes I would be making my first passenger drop off and getting paid for the first time as a cabbie.

As I was approaching where I thought the exit was, I turned on my right turn signal and began to navigate to the right lane expecting to make exit and move down the ramp straight to the destination. I turned into the right lane and suddenly it hit me------"-where is the exit? What happened? Oh my!"

By this time I had slowed down and noticed that the exit was about 100 feet behind me.. My Passenger seemed to be unaware of what had happened. So I told him with a voice full of embarrassment and regret.

'Sir, I missed the exit. Please have patience with me because today is my first day as a cab driver."

He muttered some words in his language and then said in English

'Can you find a way to get me to McCormick Place North?"

"Oh yes I can." I assured him as I began moving slowly up the ramp to I-55 not knowing exactly where I was going. Then it occurred to me to call the Dispatch with my cab radio

"Cab 952 calling."

"Yes, cab 952 can I help you?" a male voice asked.

"Yes, I missed the exit ramp to McCormick Place North and I don't know how to get back to LSD."

'What,' how long have you been driving?", 'he asked incredulously.

'Today".'I replied.

'Uh, you're a rookie? It's okay; where are you now?"'

'I am driving up the ramp heading to I-55"

'Good. Now make the first exit to State street"

After a short pause I informed him that I can see the exit.

'Good, now make a right on State Street. Then go to

Roosevelt and make another right to LSD. You should be good."

'Thank you so much." as I hung up the mic.

I eventually got my passenger to his destination. I asked him to pay me any amount that that justified the poor service I gave him. Surprisingly he paid me the meter amount with some tip.

I drove straight back to the Hyatt Regency cab stand and queued up. I was still scared to venture into the Loop and the entire downtown area because I was still intimidated by the one way streets configuration. I never really got familiar with downtown streets until I began my chauffeur license course at Harold Washington College on Lake Street. During the course I had attempted to get familiar with the Loop's one way streets,but often made wrong turns and these happened on Sundays when the Loop's traffic was virtually at about 30%of the usual traffic. So being a rookie and a novice, I avoided any ride that would take me into the Loop. Besides I did not want to ridicule the image of cab drivers who are supposed to know the streets of Chicago better than the average Chicagoan.

The Hyatt Regency hotel's cab line was moving a bit slower than it was when I came earlier to pick my first fare. So I took time out to stretch myself. I also picked a conversation with the driver directly behind me. I shared with him my ordeal with my first fare this morning and he encouraged me after he had had a good laugh about the incident. He too shared his own first day experience and asserted that every rookie driver was bound to face those challenges during the first four days on the road as a cabbie. The only exception, he said, might be drivers who were born in Chicago or those who have lived and driven on Chicago roads for many years.

He then gave me some very valuable tips. According to him there are four quarters of cab activity every work day in Chicago. First quarter, he said, is the Morning Rush Hour which begins actively around 5:30 am and ends around 8:30 am. It is one of the busiest time for cabbies especially around all the train stations in downtown where cabbies pick up workers coming to work from their various Chicago land suburbs.

The second quarter begins around 11:30am and ends around 1:30pm. Cab activity in this quarter is relatively minimal because by this time many cabs have left the city streets and are either queuing up in hotel cab stands waiting to pick up airport fares. Or have driven empty to the airports. The few cab drivers left would be seen crisscrossing downtown streets picking up workers going to the restaurants for their lunch break or those returning to their offices.

3:30 pm marks the beginning of another busy quarter-------- the third quarter. This quarter, according to him, is the afternoon rush hour. Workers are beginning to stream in their hundreds toward the train station and cabbies are busy yet again picking up from their offices and dropping off at their various train stations. A lot of patience is required from cabbies during this quarter so as not to hit a pedestrian. The pedestrians at this time seem to be impatient with the traffic lights as they hurry to catch their trains. This quarter ends around 6pm and dovetails into the fourth quarter which is the time the late working officers begin to go home. Also this is the time many guests in the hotels make their ways to the various restaurants scattered all over the city for their dinner.

By this time many cab drivers on 12 hours shift would have closed for the day including some 24 hours drivers who began work very early in the morning. So at this time there are usually a concentration of cabs on the cab stand of the big hotels like Hyatt Regency, Chicago Hilton, Sheraton and Towers, Four Seasons and others.

Finlly,he gave me what I considered the most important tip of them all which helped me immensely during the first few days of my rookie experience. He advised me to always tell my fares as soon as they board my cab and tell me their destination, that I am a rookie just beginning to drive and that I would appreciate it if they would be kind enough to give me direction to their destination. I can now testify that it worked like magic. Almost all my subsequent fares were so supportive and pleased to be of help to me. Except for one man who got angry and stormed out of my cab fearing that since I did not know the direction to his destination that I might not even know how to drive.

We broke off our conversation finaly after the whistle from the doorman sounded to invite me to go and pick up. My second fare for the day was going to the north side. After he had settled down and announced his destination, I applied my new found tactic. 'Sir,' I began, 'you're my very second fare today and I am a new driver who began work just this morning. I would appreciate it sir, if you would give me direction to your destination.'

"Oh. It will be a great pleasure to be of help to you. Now hit the ramp to Lake Shore

Drive north. Take that to Irving Park and then go west. I will direct you from there."

'Thanks."

He then went on to give me another good tip. He told me that I should always take the LSD north if the destination is north east ; though he added that I might consider other routes like Clark and Lincoln if the LSD traffic is slow. I later learned that Clark and Lincoln are two alternative diagonal roads I could take if my passengers are going to the north side. Clark Street is preferable if they are going to north east, while Lincoln is preferable for north west.

I thanked him for his kind gesture and dropped him off. I drove back to downtown through Lake Shore Drive. I finally picked an O'Hare fare. This was a piece of cake for me because I was already very familiar with the O'Hare route before I even began my chauffeur license training. I dropped and headed back to downtown empty because I did not know how to get to the cab staging area or what the procedures for picking up fares from the airport were. I ended my day in downtown around 7pm barely making enough to pay for my lease and gas for the next day. That was good ! Thank God that I survived my first rookie day without any catastrophic incident.

I came to work the next day feeling a little more confident on the road. I had to change my car because it developed some cranking noise from one of the front wheels. It was another Chevy Caprice, but a little lower mileage. I asked the cashier why he could not give me one of the newer cabs I had seen in the parking lot. He told me that I was a rookie still on probation and so until after three months of clean driving records then I could be considered for an upgrade on the type of car that I can lease.

The time was about 6:30am ; I drove for the first time to Madison street Metra train station cab stand and found it fully loaded with cabs. I drove past and turned left on Clinton and left on Monroe and headed east on Monroe. I was now beginning to unravel the one way streets quagmire of downtown. I discovered that the one way streets alternate one another. For example, all streets running east west within the Loop, beginning from Lake street, which is furthest north of the Loop, is one way east. Randolph a block south of Lake runs west. Randolph is followed by Washington which runs east while Madison runs west. Monroe runs east while Adams runs west and so on.

On the other hand, streets running north south have two streets --------State and LaSalle streets that are two way streets while the rest ------Franklin, Wells, Clark, Dearborn and Wabash run one way in alternating order. I also discovered that some streets running north south like Clark, Dearborn and Wabash at one point after the Loop change to a two way street. Clark and Dearborn turn to a two way street on Walton street while Wabash becomes a two way street after Lake street. Likewise three streets running east west namely :Randolph, Monroe and Jackson turn into a two way street after Michigan Avenue while Van Buren which runs one way west turns into a two way at Canal street.

Now armed with my new found knowledge of the downtown streets configuration, I was no more scared of driving into the Loop and downtown. My confidence grew exponentially, even though I was a little scared of picking up fares going a little farther from downtown. I picked another O'Hare airport fare while just running the streets. This time I was determined to find the airport cab staging area at O'Hare so that I would not need to drive back to downtown empty. As we got close to the airport terminals my passenger, a man, surprisingly asked if I was a new driver. I answered in the affirmative, wondering in my mind what I must have done wrong. Then I asked how he knew that. He cracked a little smile and then said that I did not add the one dollar extra charge on airport rides on the meter. I confessed to him that I did not know that and thanked him for his honesty.

After dropping him off I waited for one of the cab drivers who was also dropping off so that I could follow him to the staging area. On arriving at the staging ground I was astounded by the sheer number of Yellow cabs,checkers and other smaller cab companies represented by their colors. There must be about 400 cabs. It was just a sea of yellow cabs. These did not include the tens of black stretch limo cars which lined up in their wing of the staging ground.

I alighted from my cab primarily to use the restroom and stretch myself. Meanwhile, I asked the driver I followed to the staging ground what the procedures were in order to pick up fares from the airport. He asked if I was a new driver and I said yes.. He said I needed to go and buy the MPEA stamps because without it I cannot be allowed to pick up. After I had bought the stamps from the city vending clerks at the staging ground,

I needed to drive through the vending machines located on the lanes leading to the airport terminals to collect the airport ticket when it is the turn of my lane to drive to the terminal to pick up. The stamp is to be affixed on the ticket and submitted to the Dispatcher at the terminal. When he had concluded and I had clearly understood him I thanked him.

I locked my cab and headed to the kiosk to buy the stamps as well as use the restroom.

There were so many drivers around. Some congregated in groups chatting and enjoying some fun. Others were buying and eating their fast food purchased from the fast food restaurants and vending machines around. Some others were just walking to and fro the length of the ground which was about two hundred yards long and about one hundred yards wide, as a kind of exercise.

I started back to my cab after I had bought the stamps and used the restroom, but discovered that I had no idea where I had parked my cab. Unlike the last cab I drove yesterday I did not memorize the number. All I can tell was that it was a yellow Chevy Caprice. Of course there were hundreds of yellow cabs on the ground and a lot of them were Chevy Caprice.

"Oh my God, how do I find my cab," I lamented. Panic had started to take hold of me. I do not even have any distinguishing mark on it or in it that could help me identify it. I began frantically to look at all the yellow Chevy Caprice on the ground from row to row.

I had spent about fifteen minutes doing this when I noticed a yellow Chevy Caprice standing alone on a moving lane. I ran to it and tried my key on it and it opened the door.

I quickly jumped in and found my dairy and pen on the console. That was a great relief.

I drove quickly to catch up with the last cab on my lane before the next lane took over.

I learned a rookie lesson in a very unlikely manner: you never leave your cab on the staging ground without taking note of the lane on which you are parked. A cab can literally get 'lost' on this vast ground that is always filled with hundreds of cabs at any given time specially when airport pick ups are slow. Usually on a slow day it takes about two hours waiting time. But on some other good days or time, it could be a drive through.

I then began to understand why many cab drivers head to O'Hare airport after the morning rush hour. Usually they come to O'Hare to exercise, read (for those who are students), sleep or eat while waiting to pick up fares.

Chapter 2

HOW I BECOME A CABBIE

It is now six months I became a cabbie. I have become more comfortable and confident driving on Chicago roads. I have also begun to enjoy the job; no more tensed or fidgety feelings or attitudes. I have grown in my knowledge of the city especially learning many of the minor and hard to find streets in downtown. Streets like New----yes, New street------a small street less than 300 feet off Illinois by Mc Clurg Court.

Rush Street ------ an important street that runs one way north from Ohio street to State street. It is at the peak where State and Rush ----- two streets that run parallel to each other----- intersect to form the notorious 'Viagra Triangle' Some of the city's popular restaurants like Hugo, Gibson's Carmine, Morton's,Tarern On Rush are located on Rush street. Also some of the ladies high brow stores as well as the city's most popular bars are located on Rush. Another minor street is Dewitt Place, a street that is invaluable to cabbies to get back to

Michigan Avenue after dropping off passengers at John Hancock,

Westin and Raphael hotels on Delaware. This is because Mies Van Der Rohe street which itself is very important connecting street to Drake,Knickerbocker and Residence hotels from the Lake Shore Drive via Chicago Avenue is a one way street north from Walton Street to Pearson street.

It was on this Mies Van Der Rohe street that I was heading to Chestnut Street when a man standing with a suitcase in front of Museum of Contemporary Arts flagged me down and announced that he was going to United Airlines O'Hare airport.

I rejoiced in my heart and thanked the Lord for the fare. Picking an O'Hare ride is always the desire of any cabbie. Getting an O'Hare passenger means a guaranteed of at least sixty dollars. I noticed that my passenger was the outgoing type because he was quick to pick up a friendly conversation with me. I learned that he was a college professor in English Literature who had visited some African universities for some exchange programs. When he knew that I was a Nigerian he was very excited and wanted to know If I had read Chinua Achebe's classic novel, "Things Fall Apart". I told him I had not only read it, but had taught it in Nigerian High Schools as English literature teacher. He got more excited and interested in knowing more about me.

'So you were a high school teacher in your home country before you came to the USA?'

He asked.

'Yes, I have a bachelor's degree in English and

a masters in Curriculum Studies with emphasis on Teaching English As A Second Language,' I informed him.

'Why then are you driving cab when we need you to teach English Literature from the

African perspective in our Community Colleges, or teach English as a second language to some schools for new immigrants ?".

I told him it was never my choice to become a cab driver, but that it was the prevailing circumstance in my family that forced me to make the decision to drive cab for a living.

I came to the USA with my four young children, ages 3 to 9 years in the early nineties to join my wife who had come in 1990 with a contract to work as a registered nurse in one of Chicago's hospitals. She worked the night shifts. She usually leaves the house for work around 10pm. And comes back in the morning at about 8am and goes to sleep almost immediately. My four children were in grades 5, 4 and 3---the last one was a special need child so was in a special education school. It was an arduous task for me to take care of them all, all on my own. I did not have to do this back home in my country because I had two maids, including my sister and mom who were more than enough to take care of them. I cooked, did the laundry and dishes as well as prepare them for school in the morning and take them to school. Then at about 1.30 pm I would go get them home from school. So I was almost like a house husband of some sort to my family.

My family financial situation took a hit after my wife

and I made a drastic decision to transfer our 3 children to a private Christian School because we were not satisfied with the Public school they were assigned to attend. My wife was well paid as a nurse, but the cost of running the home and maintaining three kids in a private primary school was more than her pay could carry.

I had been looking for a job and there were jobs available, but the problem was that I could not find one that allowed for flexible time of work. Not the regular time schedule but the one that could allow me to go to work late in the morning and close late in the evening. Such jobs were nowhere to be found. And time was in the essence because we had begun to be late in our school fees payment even with overtime my wife was working. The School Principal arranged to spread the fees around the months of the school session, yet we still fell short. I needed to begin to contribute something to our family finances to augment my wife's pay. I even sold ice cream in trucks with the Alexander Ice Cream Company. That helped for just a season. So this was the financial situation in my family when a friend who was himself a cab driver suggested that I could enroll in one Harold Washington College in downtown and be trained as a cab driver.

I could not believe that I needed to go to college to be trained as a taxi driver. In my country if one wants to drive a taxi all one needs is a registered commercial car, driver's license and a knowledge of the city or town and off one goes. My friend reminded me that here is not my home country, but America where economic activities and life in general are better organized and regulated.

It did not take long time to make my decision to go for the chauffeur license training to become a cab driver.

'Oh, nobody can fault you for that; you did what you needed to do for the interest of your children and the family,' my passenger who had been listening quietly to me acknowledged. 'I hope your children will appreciate that in the future.'

We were almost close to the terminals so we drove the rest of the way to United Airlines terminal in silence. I pulled up at his terminal and he paid me and we exchanged pleasantries and good bye.

As I drove to the staging area, I began to reminisce about my training as a licensed chauffeur. I remembered how humbled I felt to find myself in a class of about sixty men and two women of different ages and from different background and countries of the world. This class was dominated by Asians, Arabs and Africans. The Asians were dominated by the Indians and Pakistanis. while the black Africans were dominated by Nigerians. There were a good number of Arabs and it was not easy to identify their countries. The two women were whites. Their accent suggested that they may have come from East European countries. I noticed that there were no American whites or African Americans and Hispanic whites among these students even though there are a small number of them among active drivers in the streets.

At first I found the course quite interesting because I was learning a lot about the city of Chicago and how to drive around it. But I did not quite put my whole mind into the course. I attended every class, but treated some of the items in the course with levity because I thought those parts of the course did not aid my knowledge of the city or how I find my destination when I eventually engage in the actual driving. The teachers were so respectful and knowledgeable about the city and all about the operation of the cab business and conducts of drivers that I thought that they must be ex cabbies.

The class was always very lively during discussion time, but the problem was that some accents were so difficult to comprehend. Some of the students seemed to have driven cabs before or have been in the classes before. I was intimidated by their knowledge of the streets and important places and locations around the city.

We were told the day for our test and from the area of the course we should expect questions. I was very confident that whatever questions they asked in the test I should be able to get 48 out of the 60 questions right. 80 percent is the minimum score for a pass.. The result of the test is released the same day of the test so that one can know if one passed or failed. We took the test and I failed. I was not surprised at all.. I knew I had problem with finding locations and addresses as well as calculating distances from one location to another. A little over half of the class passed the test. However, every student was entitled to three attempts at the test. If the student failed all three attempts he or she would be required to re-register and go through the entire course again.

I sign for my second attempt and failed again. I was really embarrassed this time and wondered why I failed because I thought I knew the questions and had made serious preparations to enable me pass.

The questions were multiple answer objective questions and students given one hour to answer the sixty questions. The answers are checked on the question sheets so there was no way to have a review of test questions in time of preparation for the test. This I suspect was designed on purpose to make the test more difficult. Well, I have one final round with the test.

I took the challenge very seriously. I made my preparations more practical than just reading and cramming the various street guides to various destinations in downtown Chicago. Every Saturday and Sunday I set out to visit downtown from my south suburb residence in the company of my cab driver friend as my tutor. We would drive all around most streets in downtown, hotels, train stations, museums, restaurants and other important places of interest.

I applied to take the exam for the third and final time. This time I was really nervous because I did not know what to expect with the type of questions that would be asked.

Would it be more difficult than the two previous tests or just the same?

I also began to doubt my decision to be a cab driver. Shouldn't I have had a little more patience while I continued to search for the job that suited my family situation?. Am I really ready to take the risks involved in driving a cab? Well, all these thoughts of doubts are no more relevant now because the bottom line is that my family needs money now and there is no guarantee that I could find the choice job soon. So I had to resist the fear of this exam and resolved to face it squarely. I had made my preparations and with some favor, I could just make it in this final test.

Well I took the exam and I did pass it. Hallelujah. Many in my class failed and will have to re-register for the course.

I must confess that the training to be a chauffeur is very rigorous and as tough as any other course in the college. Even Masters and Bachelors degree holders have failed the test three consecutive times. The course poses a very serious challenge to people who have little knowledge of Chicago roads especially those who are not familiar with downtown Chicago. For those who were born in Chicago or have lived and driven on Chicago roads before taking the course will normally have little difficulty passing the tests because the tests barely tested the would be chauffeur's knowledge of Chicago and its roads and streets.

I received my certificate and was instructed to go to Peshtigo Court----Department of Consumer Services-----building, to collect my temporary chauffeur license. I did that the next day and went the same day to Yellow Cab Company office to open an account as a driver. Yellow was the dominant cab company in Chicago then. There were other smaller companies, Yellow outnumbered all of them put together.

Chapter 3

HEY CABBIE, YOU'RE A PRO
-------DRIVE LIKE ONE

Picked up this fare at the front of the Art Institute as I headed south on Michigan Ave. She was well dressed and elegant lady. She informed me that she was going for an appointment at an address on south Wabash Street, but did not remember the number.

She knew exactly where it was located between 13th and 14th Streets So I turned right on Adams and a left on Wabash and headed south. I was doing between 25 to 30 mph and I advised her to let me know as soon as we get close to the address. After we passed

13th Street I began to slow down in anticipation for her call to stop. Instead she realized that she might have been wrong in her estimation that the address was between 13th and 14th Streets instead of15th and 16th Streets. So I continued towards 15th Street and suddenly she shouted " stop! Stop!! stop!!! Just on impulse, I instantly pulled over to the right and stopped. I realized immediately after I had stopped, that that was a bad driving.

First, I should have been mindful of the car following behind me. I did not show any indication with my directional pointer that I was pulling over to the right neither did I slow down before stopping. And before I could finish my thought sure enough a car was following right behind me ------ an unmarked Chicago Police Department car stopped with a screeching sound as the officer braked to avoid making contact with my cab rear bumper. Immediately the dreaded police blue flashing light came on.

I told my passenger that the police had caught me. She honestly admitted she was responsible.

The officer stepped out of his car and walked majestically towards my cab. He stood by my door, stooped and said through the window. 'Hey cabbie, you're a pro, why not drive like one. Do you realize what your violation is?'

'Yes sir, I do; it's my passenger -------'

'Officer, please it was my fault.' My passenger interjected trying to save me from getting a ticket.

'Ma'am, he is a pro; he should know better.'

He collected my driver's license and went back to his car.

My passenger apologized again as she paid me and left to keep her appointment. This ticket would be my first ticket from the police after nearly one year as a cab driver. I had prided myself as a very careful driver even before I began driving the cab. I tried as much as possible to obey traffic rules. I hated speeding. I believe that driving above 65 mph is not safe. Anything can happen at this speed if there is a slight loss of concentration on the road. I usually maintain a speed of 60 mph on local expressways and highways with a posted speed limit of 55 mph. I have learned from experience that the cops do not bother you if you are above the speed limit by about 5 miles or less.

On highways with 65 mph speed limit, I was usually fagged out each time I make a long trip on them. This is because of the high level concentration required from me to drive at that speed. Even at that speed other cars, trucks and trailers would be literally flying past me.

But on local roads and streets, no driver, I repeat no driver, obeys the speed limit.

I don't either. That is why I believe that the cops can always issue speeding ticket to all drivers on the roads at any given time if they have the means to do that. Every driver on Chicago roads exceeds the posted speed limits on our roads. They only slow down whenever cops are detected to be sneaking around the road to catch speeders. That's why whenever I am on Lake Shore Drive north or south bounds, particularly north bound I am usually very alert watching my rear view mirror to make sure that no cop is following me. But on the south LSD, their hunting spots are well known to drivers and they are usually easily detected. During the nights I usually maintain the speed limits of 40 mph for north and 45mph for south because there is no art to know which head lamps belong to a cop in the night.

The Police Officer came back with the ticket and after explaining what I should do with the ticket, handed it to me. I drove off, but could not shake off the memory of his cold but mild rebuke of my driving. 'Hey cabbie, you're a pro, drive like one.'

I was really upset by this ticket. I needed to calm my nerves down before continuing work. I drove to Yellow Cab garage, parked and remained in my cab while I ruminated on the violation ticket. It was all my fault for allowing my driving to be controlled by the passenger. I should have been in complete control of my actions on the wheels and not be dictated to by what my passenger said or did from the back seat. That was what the cop meant when he berated me : 'You're a pro, drive like one.'

If I had driven like a professional as the cop said, maybe I shouldn't have received this ticket. So there and then I made a resolution that I will never again allow my driving to be influenced by the instructions or opinions from my fares. 'I am going to be my kind of driver henceforth.' I declared pounding my fist on the passenger's seat.

My resolution was challenged three weeks later when I picked up a young lady from the O'Hare airport. As soon as this young lady entered the cab she said: 'Driver, I am in a hurry; I must be in downtown Chicago in 20 minutes.'

'Good day ma'am,' I said trying to sound professional, 'I will try to get you to downtown as soon and safe as possible, but I will not drive outside the bounds of traffic rules.'

'Just get me there as fast as possible'

'I will ma'am,' I replied as I drove off.

I was firm in my resolve that I would not drive under any pressure from this woman.

I would maintain my composure and be very respectful in my responses to whatever she said or did. I must not get another ticket because of pressure to please my passenger.

After all, the violation would go to my driving record and she would not assist in the payment of the financial penalty that would be involved.

The traffic was good and I was already driving my maximum on local highway—60 mph.

'Driver, you're slow; can you go faster?'

'Ma'am I 'm doing 62 mph on a 55mph road. That's the fastest I can go.'

'Oh my gosh, why do I have to be driven by this jerk?' she said under her breath,but well intended that I hear it.

'I 'm not a jerk ; I'm only a cabbie with a keen desire for safety which comes from obedience to traffic rules. If I get pulled over by the cops you will not get the ticket on your driving record, but mine. And will not help with paying the financial penalty.'

She got my message. She eventually gave up trying to force me to drive to her taste.

So we drove the rest of the way in silence. When we got to her destination at north Dearborn, we pulled into a residential apartment building and not an office so I began to wonder what the rush was for her to get back to her residence.

I was elated by my first victory over an overbearing passenger who wanted to drive the cab from the back seat. There are not many of this type of passenger among the riding public. Most cab riders do not like speedy cabbies. A good example was this elderly lady I picked up at the Midway airport who on entering my cab told me pleadingly that she would appreciate it if I did not speed. I assured her that I was not a speeder and that I actually hated speeders. I promised her that she would enjoy my driving.

Our trip from Midway to downtown Chicago was very relaxed and friendly. She told a lot about her family; her four children---2boys and 2 girls,who were all married and living with their own families. Her 2 sons-in-laws and 2 daughters-in-law. Her grand children some of whom she was unable to keep up with remembering their birthdays.

She also revealed that she was returning from her first son's place in Florida. She had gone to see her latest the grand son who was born the previous month. I could see from my rear view mirror that she was relaxed and happy with my driving.

As we pulled into the drive way of her apartment she smiled and asked for my work phone number so that she could always call me any time she would be going to or returning from the airport. She also confessed that she had never enjoyed her previous cab rides as much as she enjoyed this ride. She handed me a 50 dollar bill and as I reached to my pocket to give her change she told me to keep it. I couldn't be happier that this lady enjoyed her ride.

My resolution to drive like a pro is not restricted to my desire to stop my passengers from interfering with my driving, but included my compliance with all traffic

27

rules of the road. So I made a point of duty as a pro to obey all traffic rules. More so after I had attended the mandatory 8 hours safe driving classes. I gained some better understanding of some of the traffic rules especially the stop signs. I used to be one of those that slow down and then roll across the stop signs. I don't usually make a complete stop just like about 75% of other driver do. Yes, only about 25% of drivers really make a complete stop at the stop signs. I can support my claim with the unscientific study I personally conducted about this sometime in 2002. This was how this study was conducted. I stood at a fairly busy 3 ways intersection with stop signs at the three corners of the intersection Armed with my pen and a note book I made a record of all drivers who used this intersection within one hour 36 minutes it took to record 100 vehicles. Of all the 100 vehicles I recorded 12 drivers made a complete stop. 13 drivers slowed down and stopped because a driver had arrived earlier than they did. 51 drivers slowed down and slowly rolled on. 21 drivers slowed down and then drove on. 3 drivers made no attempt to slow down or stop. Out of these 3, 2 were trucks. So I resolved with myself that as a pro I must be counted as one of those drivers who obeyed the rules of the roads. This is not to say that I have not received a ticket for not stopping at a stop sign. In fact I did receive a ticket in 2001.The fact was that I was on unfamiliar road and it was in the night in a poorly lit road with a truck standing at the corner of the road. After this ticket I began as a precautionary measure to be stopping at every intersection when I 'm in doubt or when I' m on an unfamiliar roads. I stop at every stop sign even when the road is dark and lonely. I recall one weekend I was returning from work at about 1 o'clock in the morning. From the major road to my street is about half a mile and there are 6 stop signs. On this very night the road was quiet and lonely. A car was following me as I drove home. As I got to the first stop sign I did a complete stop. The second and third stop signs I did the same thing. I was approaching the 4th stop sign when suddenly, the car sped past and the driver shouted some expletives at me as he drove past me and the stop sign. I watched him as he drove through the 5th and the 6th stop signs as if they never existed there.

Not long ago I picked a young lady from downtown Chicago who was going to the north side. This was during the afternoon rush hour. She gave me her choice of route. That was to go through Clybourn to Belmont and from Belmont she would direct me how to go from there.

As soon as we took off I immediately sensed that she was the impatient back seat driver instructor. She cursed beneath her breath any time I made a complete stop at the stop sign and would yell any time we are approaching a green light, 'you must make that light.' And if I failed to make the green light and stopped at the yellow she would scream and curse louder. At one point I really got offended, but when I looked at her from my rear view mirror I noticed that she looked very agitated and red on the face I restrained myself. As we approached the next light she warned again that I must make the green light, but unfortunately I did not increase my speed in order to make the green light. So we did not make the green light again. I stopped as soon as the yellow light appeared.

If it were in the past may be, I could have, but not any more since the arrival of the red light cameras installed by the city at most intersections. I have learned to quit trying to make the green light by running the yellow light. I got two red light camera tickets and had paid two hundred dollars in fines.

As a driver who is safety conscious I had applauded the introduction of the red light cameras because I believe they saved some lives and prevented some costly accidents on some dangerous intersections in the city. In fact some cabbies got as many as three tickets in one day. And usually nobody wins when they contest them. The video and photo evidences were always there to prove the camera right. Those cameras indeed curtailed the excesses of some irresponsible cabbies.

So I asked my irritated passenger as politely as I could 'Ma'am do you drive on Chicago roads?'

'Yes I do, but I don't drive like my grand mother.'

'How many hundreds of dollars, If I may ask, have you paid to the city of Chicago for red light tickets?'

'It's none of your business,' she replied.

I sensed I should deliver the coup de grace.

'You see what I mean? I had paid two hundred dollars in 45 days to the city of Chicago for red light tickets and I have the choice not to pay that anymore by not speeding up to make the green light when it is not possible. And more over the stop signs say to stop and not to slow down or roll across. You have been mad with me because I have refused to drive like you and not obey the rules. I am sorry to offend you, but that's how I have decided to do my job.'

'But there were no cameras there!', she protested.

I kept mum and we drove in silence all the way to her destination. As she stepped out of my cab she said: 'You're the worst cab driver that has ever driven me home and because of that I will withhold your tip.' She handed me the exact meter amount.

'Thanks for your business,' I said with tongue-in-cheek attitude as she walked away," and may your next cabbie be your type of driver.'

Chapter 4

CHICAGO CABBIES

They have come to America from every corner of the world in pursuit of a better life for themselves and their families. Dozens of countries of the world are represented in the Chicago cabbies community. They are from Afghanistan, Angola, Argentina, Arabs from North Africa, and the Middle East, Belarus, Brazil, Burkina Faso, Bosnia, Cameroon, Chad, Chile, China, Congo, Croatia, Ethiopia, Gambia, Gabon, Ghana, Haiti India, Ivory Coast, Kenya, Liberia, Nigeria, Pakistan, Philippine, Poland, Russia, Serbia, Senegal, Somalia, Sudan, Togo, Uganda and Zambia. Of course there are the native born Americans, but it is worthy of note that over 90% of cabbies are first generation immigrants from the above countries. They are hard workers who believe in the dignity of labor. Over 60% of them are married with children and they work hard to provide for their families. From my own estimation the average age of Chicago cabbies is about 40 years and these are family oriented men and women. Only about less than 1% of cabbies are women.

Most cabbies are predominantly from developing countries of the world or as they are often called, the third world countries of Africa Asia, Middle East and some East European countries. They are very well educated. Thousands of cabbies have undergraduate degrees from universities here or from their home countries before coming here in search of a better life. It is highly believed that Chicago cab drivers are one of the highly educated professional groups in Chicago.

Some part time cab drivers are government workers, university students and other labor groups who want some quick cash for school fees, family financial obligation and other expenditure their regular salaries could not carry.

There are about 18000 cabbies driving about 7000 cabs on the streets of Chicago.

To a casual observer it would seem sometimes that there are too many cabs operating on Chicago roads, but let there be an event that attracts just a hand full of thousands of people into Chicago then it becomes difficult to find available cabs. Chicago cannot do without a high presence of cabs on her streets. In the first place, it is a center of state government activities. The state and city offices, and that of Cook County are headquartered in Chicago. Don't forget that numerous local and international companies are based in Chicago also.

Another is the fact that the cost of parking in Chicago is very exorbitant. Many people who work or do business in Chicago from the suburbs prefer, for economic reasons, to drive their cars to various train stations in their suburb, park there and come to the city by train. These kind of workers find the cabs invaluable in their movement in downtown

Chicago.

Chicago cabbies are usually on the road for an average of 12 hours a day. Some of the younger ones like the students and some of the part time cabbies drive for over 15 hours a day. They begin work around 5 am and work till 8 or 9 pm. And if it is on the weekend they could work for much more hours. They specialize in the lease program called the 'Weekend Special' The weekend special is a lease program where the daily lease driver or the part time driver can lease a cab for three consecutive days---

Friday, Saturday and Sunday. So a cab driver who signs for this special lease would want to make every use of his time to make money.

There are four categories of cab drivers in Chicago cab industry. The 12 and 24 hours lease, weekly lease and the owner operators program. The 24 hours lease grants the cabbies the use of the cab for 24 hours. This is renewable every morning. Majority of cabbies operate this kind of lease program because it affords them the privilege to use the car even when they are not on duty. The 12 hours lease program is dominated by student cabbies, part time cabbies or cabbies who make cab driving a second job. The 12 hours shift drivers are always in a hurry on the roads. The adage that 'time is money' rings perfectly correct with them. They are very aggressive in the pursuit of fares. Some of them in my opinion,, are one of the worst and reckless drivers on the streets. You can always tell their arrival to duty after 6 pm when the tempo of cabs movement shoots up everywhere in downtown.

The weekly lease is the most comfortable lease than the 12 and 24 hours lease program in the sense that it affords the leaser the right to keep and work with the car for a week.

This is renewable every week. Some cab companies allow two cabbies to lease a cab for a week and they both share in the use and payment of the lease.

Owner operator program was already in place when I became a cabbie 17 years ago.

This is a program that lets the cabbie assume the ownership of the car (usually a new car) and is required by the agreement he signed to have the responsibility of the maintenance of the car as well as make the required weekly payments. This weekly payment goes on until he pays off the cost of the car according to the number of years stipulated in the agreement. Then, depending on the agreement, he might want to buy off the car for private use.

I became an owner operator in April 1996,and received a new 1996 Chevy Lumina.

After 3 years I was able to complete the payment of the car and Yellow Cab Company sold the car to me at $2000. That was in the agreement I signed. This car served me and my family well because all my three children used the car through out their high school days.

Chicago cab drivers are one of the most maligned

professional service providers in Chicago. Even though they provide a lot of thankless services to the city residents and visitors, they are often never appreciated. There are always complaints against cab drivers: they are rude and disrespectful to passengers; they drive dirty and smelly cabs.

They are reckless and careless on the road. They refuse services to certain passengers going to certain parts of the city. There is no doubt that some cab drivers may be guilty of these charges, but majority of cab drivers in Chicago are good, honest and respectful professionals who take their job very seriously. The general public should not allow the irresponsible action of a few bad eggs to color their perception of the cabbies community. Just like in any group of good people there are always the bad ones, so it is with cab drivers. Even the Lord Jesus Christ had a bad egg among His twelve disciples and that did not negate the good work the rest of the Apostles did. Does the presence of a few bad cops negate the good work the Chicago Police Department do to protect us and maintain law and order? I quite agree that there are really some bad cab drivers out there and that is the reality of life.

Somebody may ask what other jobs do cab drivers do other than pick up passengers and drop them at their destinations. Well, you may have to ask the people who are unable to find their way in and around Chicago downtown who they go to for direction. Or the visitor who is just feeling his way around the city who he goes to for guides. Chicago cabbies do not only act as personal tour guides to visitors they are also able ambassador to the city. So personally I usually feel obligated to do everything within my power to give any visitor or any one indeed, direction to his destination. Some time if I sense that mere word description might not make enough sense, I usually, if I don't have a fare, volunteer to let the visitor drive behind me as I take him to the address. There is usually no better good feeling of satisfaction that beats this.

I recall on one occasion a visitor to downtown got her car towed for illegal parking. She and her friend stopped me on Canal Street as I was turning into Washington Street and asked for direction to the City's Auto Pound on lower East Wacker Drive. From where they stopped me there was no way they could locate the Auto Pound even with the best description. So I just decided that the best I could do for them was to take them there.

So I told them to follow me. I took them to the Auto Pound and as I was driving away she honked at me. I stopped and she ran to me and handed me a ten dollar bill. 'Thank you very much for your kindness.' She said.

Many visitors to Chicago have adored and praised the city for two notable things. One, the beauty and cleanliness of the city.. And secondly, the friendliness and kindness of the city residents and they have always promised to come back again. Chicago cab drivers contributed in no small measure for this praise accorded to the people of Chicago.

The Chicago cabbie is not only expected to know everywhere in Chicago, he is also supposed to be a compendium of knowledge about everything Chicago. For example, he is supposed to know every historical fact about Chicago so as to be able to communicate the same to inquiring visitors to Chicago. He is supposed to know that the city was incorporated in 1837 and that the first city resident was a black man called Jean Baptiste Du Sable who built the first settlement in Chicago in 1779. That the notorious Chicago fire occurred in October 8th 1871, from the cow barn of one Mr. Patrick O'Leary. The only surviving structures in the entire city that escaped the destruction of the great fire are the two gothic architectural water tower building along Michigan Ave and Chicago Ave. That one Pablo Picasso was the one who sculptured and erected in 1967,the 162 ton steel sculpture on Daley Plaza in downtown.

A cursory look at the cabbies community will reveal that cabbies came from virtually everywhere in the world particularly from poor countries of Africa, Asia and from the Arab world. They are usually well educated and are first generation immigrants to America. The question is why is it that cab business is attractive to them when they are eligible by their educational qualification to get employed elsewhere. Some of them are lawyers, engineers, teachers, bankers,business administrators and other fields. I think

I can proffer some explanations. First generation immigrants may be inhibited by their accent which sometime makes them unable to communicate effectively with the average American. Second reason is that some of them who obtained their degrees from universities in their home countries have degrees that are not highly regarded by employers here. The most likely reason, in my opinion,why cab business is attractive to new immigrants from mostly poor countries is because of the allure of being independent and self employed. This is coupled by the fact that it does not require a lot of capital and high educational qualification to become a cab driver or start a cab business. All that is needed is a Chicago city chauffeur's license and a valid Illinois driver's license and he's ready to go and make money. No boss to answer to; start work at his own time and end at his own time.

Even though cabbies compete hard in pursuit of fares on the streets, they enjoy a close professional fraternity. A cabbie will always stop to help a fellow cabbie if there is any break down on the road due to flat tire or weak battery that needs jump starting. Cabbies have developed some hand signals they exchange among themselves to inform one another if for example, there is a police presence on a particular road checking for speeders or any other violation. It's thumb down. If the road is all clear, it's thumb up.

Cabbies also inform one another through the dispatch to avoid a particular road when there is a traffic jam as a result of an accident.

In the nineties before the introduction of the 'bullet' shield for cabbies protection, cabs were fitted with two red top light on each side of the cab dome light cover. These two red top light begin to blink as soon as the floor distress call switch (usually installed on the drivers side of the floor) is activated with the foot of the driver. In those days for cabbies' safety each cab was installed with this emergency distress call switch which the cabbie can activate if he is in any danger. When activated an alarm is sent to the dispatch and the dispatch calls the police and informs them of the location of the cab.

While this is going on, the two red light at the each side of the of the dome light cover begin to blink That's a signal to fellow cabbies that a buddy is in some kind of danger.

Cabbies are required to check on their buddy whenever they see a stationary cab with blinking red dome light.

It used to be very dangerous to drive cabs in the nineties. I remember when I began to drive in 1996, there were about six cabbies killed in robbery attacks that year. And that was the period many cab drivers began to refuse services to those going to far south and west sides especially to young black men and women.

Cabbies fraternity is also extended to cabbie on cabbie accidents. If for instance two cabs are involved in an accident where no one was injured and the damage is minor, both cabbies will reach a settlement acceptable to both. It will not be reported to the police or to the insurance. The culprit will admit his guilt and would be responsible for the repair of both cabs. Both cabbies would then head to the mechanic workshop where the repairs are quickly done. If on the other hand there is no mutual agreement on who was responsible for the accident then they may then go to the police. But many times if the damage is minor, both cabbies repair their cabs and move on because time is money.

There are special cab cars mechanics in downtown, who exclusively serve cab drivers and do rarely work on private cars. These mechanics charges are relatively moderate in comparison to what is charged elsewhere. And more importantly their services are quick. A job that might take a whole day in other mechanic workshops might just take a couple of hours with them. And these mechanics are aware that time is money to cabbies so they try to attend to cabbies as quick as possible so as to continue to enjoy their patronage.

Even though cab drivers enjoy a good professional fraternity, one thing that has eluded them is the ability to unite together under one professional umbrella to fight for a common cause. That is the reason why most of the strikes or work stoppages calls by the leaders are mostly unsuccessful. There are too many splinter groups among cabbies and also because of the nature of the operation of the business. It is not often possible to get cabbies together for a meeting because there is the problem of the 12 and 24 hours lease drivers who would be unable to pay for their lease if they spend their valuable time in a meeting or on strike. So usually only a handful of independent owners, owner operators and weekly lease drivers that can afford to participate in a work stoppage or strike. Added to this problem is the fact that cab companies do not cooperate with cabbies because such actions like strikes affect their revenue. Perhaps the only way of solving Chicago cabbies disunity is for them to hire the services of a labor activist to unionize the Chicago Cab Drivers Association into a strong viable labor union.

Religion is one strand that unites Chicago cab drivers especially among the moslems. Moslems from all parts of the world congregate together to worship and pray during their prayer time. The Moslem cabbies sometime drive empty to O'Hare or Midway airports in order to join in their congregational prayer time during their holy months.

It looks like the City gave the Moslems a tacit approval to take over the O'Hare airport cabbies common room as a prayer room, especially during the winter. The City even installed a specialized wash basin and tap for their pre - prayer purification rituals.

This is quite commendable of the City of Chicago. But the irony is the fact that these moslems who enjoy this unqualified freedom of worship here in Christian America are those whose home countries burn churches, kill and persecute Christians for exercising their faith in those countries.

Christian Cabbies do not have any congregational meeting any where, but their presence is only noticed at the bill boards in both airports. There you would see their various church invitation cards and hand bills inviting all to their programs. There is one popular South Korean cabbie whose presence at the airports is always noticed whenever he is at the airports. This is because he would walk the entire rolls of cab lanes several times preaching and appealing to all to accept Jesus Christ as their Savior, because His return to earth is imminent. He also sometime shared Christian tracts.

There is also the Jehovah Witness cabbie who walks around at the airport distributing free religious materials to fellow cabbies. As far as I know there has never been a religious conflict among cabbies; everyone respects one another.

Chapter 5

CRAZY CABBIES

While I was still undergoing the chauffeur license training course at the Harold Washington College on Lake Street, I had a habit of visiting downtown every Saturday of the month to site- see as well as try to familiarize myself with the city. I normally take the train from my south suburban residence to downtown and then walk around the Loop and its streets and then walk to the near north side and back to the train station.

On one occasion I arrived downtown as usual via the train and walked up to the street level from the Randolph Street train station. I walked up the steps of the Cultural Center on Randolph and Michigan and stood there beside the cab stand, trying to make a mental plan on where to go. It was a sweltering hot summer day with a palpable humidity as I stood there for a moment watching people go by either arriving from the train station or going home. A cab pulled up at the cab stand in front of the Cultural Center. A

43

young black man alighted from the cab and slammed the door of the cab very hard as he muttered some angry words. Suddenly the cab driver, a young man in his late twenties, in a basketball shorts and sleeveless tee shirt and a baseball cap, jumped out from his cab to confront the passenger as he walked briskly down the stairs of the train station. When the cab driver realized that he could not catch up with him, he stopped and began to rain curses and abuses on the passenger with the most vulgar and obscene words connected with the F-word and his mother. I was appalled by the uncivilized behavior of the cab driver who, though, was angered by the slamming of his cab's door by the passenger should have had a better choice of word in the presence of the little children and seniors who were all standing or sitting in the front of the Cultural Center. I was so scandalized by this incident that I began to wonder if I really wanted to be a cab driver in this city after all. If I am, I really would not want to have this kind of cab driver as a co-worker.

I have heard tales about crazy cabbies with notoriety for reckless behavior and vulgarism among Chicago cab drivers. May be this driver is one of them.

I walked up to Michigan Avenue and headed north with the throng just site seeing. Usually my routine is to walk up north on Michigan to the end of Michigan which is Oak street. Make a left on Oak street and walk to La Salle street and then head down south to the Loop But this day I decided to go further north on La Salle street to North Avenue. When I walked to North Avenue, I was really exhausted. So I went into one of the fast food restaurants and refreshed myself. When it was time to go home I decided to take the cab because I was too tired to walk to the Randolph street train station. I boarded a cab at the corner of La Salle and North Ave. My driver was a middle aged Arab or Pakistani man, and his cab was stuffy with smell of cigarette smoke. I immediately noticed that he was smoking with the windows rolled up because the AC was on. I respectfully appealed to him to stop smoking and to let me wind down the window so that I can have some fresh air. It was as if I lit his back side with fire. He stepped on the gas and began weaving dangerously in and out of the traffic to overtake the other cars.

I was really scared so I quickly put on my seat belt.

'Driver you're moving too fast and I told you that your smoking is choking me'.

Suddenly without warning, he rammed on his brake and pulled over.

'Hey man, What do you want? You don't want me to smoke and you don't want me to drive; what do you want?'

Before I could comprehend his insensitive reaction to my request not to smoke or drive too fast, he bolted out from the cab, stepped out to the curb side and opened the right rear door where I was sitting and ordered me out of his cab.

'Leave my (F-word) cab,' he yelled at me.

I quickly stepped out and he banged the door, got into his cab and sped off.

'Wow!' I exclaimed in disbelief of what had just happened. I did not know where I was.

But I knew I was half way to Randolph Street. So I

headed south on La Salle to Randolph street and from there I made it to the train station.

O n my ride home I began to ruminate on the two incidents involving two Chicago cab drivers on the same day. I came to a quick conclusion that Chicago cabbies must be largely wild and uncultured people who are devoid of civilized behavior. I began to develop some dislike for cabbies. But when I eventually became involved with the cab business, I discovered to my amazement that most cabbies are responsible family oriented men and a few women in their forties,,fifties and sixties who respect and carry themselves with dignity and do their job in the most civilized manner.

They understand that they are in the business to make a living and provide for their families. So they carry out their work in the most professional manner so as not to jeopardize their source of livelihood.

The presence of crazy cabbies among Chicago cab drivers community has become a nuisance and aberration to the good image of Chicago cabbies. The crazy cabbies are responsible for the poor goodwill cabbies have among most of the cab riding public.

The culture of our society whereby bad and negative incidents or news are accorded prominent coverage in our news reporting, favors the unprofessional activities of the crazy cabbies. So each time the cabbies are in the news, it is always the deviant behavior of the crazy cabbies that takes preeminence and not the activities of over 95% of good Chicago cabbies who quietly, responsibly and respectfully carry out their job as cab drivers in Chicago.

Good cabbies go out of their way to provide extra

services to their passengers especially the seniors whom they treat with extra care and make them enjoy their rides by helping them with their bags and other stuffs. Volunteering sometimes to take those stuffs to their door steps or into their apartment building. They treat their fares with due courtesy even when they receive insult in return. They are not wild drivers on the streets and roads.

They do not cheat their fares in any manner. They return all forgotten items either to the Lost and Found Department or on many times go the extra mile by driving to the home or the office of the passenger who forgot the item.

Good cabbies are often dismayed and horrified by the insensitivity of crazy cabbies to the scathing criticism of the public and the rest of the cab community to their wild and unprofessional conduct as Chicago cabbies.

It is not difficult to identify crazy cabbies. They are usually young; seldom well dressed. On the road they are dangerous and reckless drivers. They speed even on busy streets and seldom have regard for traffic rules. They often run red lights and do not stop at stop signs. In fact it was the arrival of the red light camera on some intersection s in Chicago that curtailed their penchant to run red lights. Their notoriety for traffic violation in downtown is a common knowledge among residents of Chicago. Whenever you see a police car pull over a motorist for traffic violation in downtown more often than not the driver involved is usually a cabbie. And in most times 90% of the cabbies involved are the crazy cabbies.

The crazy cab drivers are so desperate and aggressive in the pursuit of passengers on the streets of downtown that they would not mind running a red light or driving against a one way street in order to beat a fellow cab driver to a fare. Sometimes if another cab is flagged down by a fare on the right curb side and a crazy cabbie happens to be on the same street, but on the left lane. The crazy cabbie would without hesitation or consideration for other drivers in the middle lane, dive diagonally to the right, in an attempt to beat the cabbie on the right lane to the fare. Some time they succeed in 'stealing' the fare.

Sometime if it is a crazy cabbie against a crazy cabbie, then watch out, because a dangerous drag race between them will ensue. Many times the fares run for their lives as the drag race dangerously approaches them.

Most Chicago cabbies hate the crazy cabbies; they are to cabbies what ruffians and miscreants are to the society. They intimidate other cabbies to submission to their will on the streets and roads. Most cabbies avoid being tempted into a drag race competition with them over fares. They rather let them win than risking a possible accident.

The crazy cabbies are usually daily lease drivers driving cabs owned either by individual owners or the big companies. They drive the cabs roughly over potholes or any other rough conditions on the roads. Sometime, they force themselves into other drivers lanes and daring the drivers to hit them. Many times those drivers yield to them to avoid an accident. If you check the driving records of most crazy cabbies, it is like a rap sheet filled with various traffic violations tickets. I wish the City introduces the 3 strikes rule here, but with a sight modification. Instead of 3 strikes for suspension, we should have 3 strikes of moving violation tickets in one year for a fine of some hundreds of dollars. Fines are more appropriate than suspension because some of the crazy cabbies may be the bread winners in their families. I believe this could help curb the excesses of crazy cabbies.

Many Chicago cab riders have their tales of uncomfortable encounters with crazy cabbies and are always ready to share them.

There was this woman I picked up at O'Hare airport ------- a short trip ride. As soon as she stepped into the cab, she began to apologize for the short trip and promising to give a good tip. I calmed her down and told her that she didn't need to apologize because short trips from the airports are part of the categories of passengers cabbies are supposed to pick up at the airport. I assured her that I was delighted to give her a ride home after a safe return flight home. She then proceeded to tell me one of the experiences she had with a cabbie the last time she took a cab from O'Hare to her residence at Cumberland and Higgins in Parkridge. She said the moment she told the driver her destination, the cabbie became visibly upset and angry. He spoke in his native language so she was unable to understand what he was saying. As they left the airport to the highway he was almost flying. She said she was scared for her life because she thought he might crash the cab.

She tried to caution him, but he pretended not to hear. Eventually she was relieved to arrive her home. The cabbie quickly got out, popped open the trunk and got out her suitcase and tossed it roughly to the ground and demanded payment. She said she only gave him just the meter amount and added no tip. This seemed to have got the cabbie madder as he slammed the door of his cab and drove off.

I told her that that driver behaved like a crazy cabbie. No normal or regular driver would take it out on the passenger for receiving a short trip fare from the dispatcher at the airport. It is not the passenger's fault that he got a short trip fare. A driver should rather blame his luck if he is given a short trip fare.

After all some driver must get the short trip fare and if it happens to be a crazy cabbie that gets it, so be it. There is no denying the fact that a driver might feel frustrated if after spending over an hour waiting at the staging area to be invited to pick up a fare at the terminal and only to be given a fare going to one of the neighborhoods close to the airport while other cabbies get fares going to downtown or some of the far suburbs. A short trip pays a driver a maximum of 15 dollars (but he is required to go back to the airport and pick up without having to wait),while to downtown or a suburb is a minimum of 40 dollars.

She agreed with me that it was wrong for cabbies to shift the frustration to the passenger who had no hand in the driver being offered a short trip fare. We arrived at her residence and she gave me a twenty dollar bill for a meter ride of 9 dollars and told me to keep the change. That was cool.

Chapter 6

CABBIES COPS AND COURTS

An adage says that it is the child that often does the dishes that is likely to break them. An average private car driver who drives his car from home to work every work day of the week and uses the same car for weekend grocery shopping and Sunday church attendance, may be on the road for about 10 hours a week. But a cabbie who drives an average of 12 hours a day could at the end of every week log in a physically and mentally exerting 84 hours of driving. Many times it is done under severe weather conditions like several inches of snow fall., or severe thunder storms and flooding. These cabbies are always on the road no matter what the road conditions are. So, that they rake in high numbers of traffic violation tickets is because of the job they do. This can be regarded as one of the hazards of being a cabbie. Not only this, cabbies are usually driving under pressure to make money every day to pay for their daily lease and provide for their families.

It is no wonder therefore, that for every 3 drivers pulled over by cops on Chicago roads, one is usually a cabbie. Some cabbies feel that because of the frequency with which they are pulled over and given a ticket, that the Cops do not like Cabbies.

The question about whether the cops hate cabbies could be answered with a question.

Do cops hate gang bangers? Yes, of course they do. Chicago Cops would rather spend their time doing some other aspects of their policing duties than risking their lives chasing after gang bangers and their murderous activities in Chicago neighborhoods. So it is inevitable that cabbies attract a closer attention from the Cop because of the recklessness of some of the cabbies on the roads.

Chicago Cabbies have poor road users image with the Chicago Cops. But some cabbies will swear with their last dime that the Cops hate cabbies. They tell about bias in the issuance of moving violation tickets by cops whenever they come upon cars on a particular road moving with the flow of traffic, but moving above the speed limit. They claim that it is usually the taxi car that is singled out and pulled over.

Some other cabbies claim that whenever there is an accident involving a cabbie that the cops often tend to take the sides of the other driver in accessing the guilty driver. I personally can say that I have been involved in this kind of alleged partiality by cops.

Many years ago, when I was relatively a few years into my cab driving experience, I was involved in an accident with a small delivery truck on Illinois street and McClough Court. I was on the left lane on Illinois street heading east. As I was approaching McClough Court, I decided to make a left into McClough, so I moved over to the turning lane, while the truck which was moving side by side with me was on the middle lane. As I was initiating my turn, it appeared that the truck was going straight towards Lake Shore Drive because there was no left turning signal on. Then suddenly the truck driver decided to make a left by initiating his turn from the center lane. By this time I had only completed half of my turn when I saw the truck bearing down on the passenger side of my cab. I quickly swerved my cab to the left into the opposing lane to avoid a direct hit on the right side of my cab.

But I could not move fast enough to avoid a contact with the truck. His rear left tail scraped the front right fender of my cab because I had to stop to avoid a collision with a car coming from the opposite direction. The truck driver stopped and was very sorry for the damage on my right fender and elected to give me some money to go fix it. I agreed, but told him that we must first of all obtain a police report. Yellow Cab Company has always insisted that drivers must obtain police report for any accident no matter how minor it might be. He complained that he had deliveries to make and that he could not go with me to the police office. I warned him of the implications and that if he decided not to go with me that I would go alone. He drove away in anger. Before he drove off I had collected his name, phone number and the name and phone number of his company.

When I got to the downtown police station there

were other drivers who were there waiting for their turn to report their accidents. I sat beside a driver who happened to be a cabbie, who also came to get a police report. He was accompanied by the driver who hit him. He told me that the driver who hit him ran the red light and that he had pledged to fix the damage on the cab. He was invited before me to give his report. While he was reporting to the police officer sitting behind the counter, I could only hear when he raised his voice to say: 'he ran the red light and hit me.'

I could not make out what the police officer was saying to him. When they were done with the officer, both collected the police report. But the cabbie was visibly angry and kept saying: 'can't believe this!'

The driver who hit him looked confused and apologetic. I asked the cabbie what transpired between them and the cop. He told me with anger in his voice. 'Could you believe that the cop said that I was the guilty driver?'

I did not have time to find out how exactly the accident happened because I was the next called to meet with another officer at another counter. Prompted by him I told him that the delivery truck driver who was involved in the accident refused to come along with me. He asked if I had his information. I told him I had his name and phone number including his company's phone number. He told me to call him or his company and inform them that the truck driver was wanted at the police office. I made the call to the truck driver and told him that the cops want him to report at their office immediately.

I also called his company and reported the accident to his manager. The manager was already defensive. He claimed that his driver never hit me. I warned him he must instruct his driver to come over to the police office or he could be charged for fleeing after an accident.

The truck driver showed up after an hour. We both stood before the cop. The truck driver gave his own account of what happened, but told nothing but lies to avoid culpability in the accident. When he was done, I told the cop that all he said were all lies. I then proceeded to narrate how the accident happened. From my observation of the attitude of the cop I began to think that the cop believed the trunk driver's account.

Then he began to cross question me in a manner that indicated to me that he was trying to make me admit that I was the one who initiated the contact just as the truck driver had lied. I protested vehemently and even pleaded with him to go out and see the car and the truck which were parked at the parking lot so he could see for himself. He refused to go outside and eventually accepted the lies of the truck driver. I could not believe that the cop could treat this accident the way he did. I was really saddened and dejected by the turn of events. Could it be that there might be some credence to the belief by cabbies that they usually receive raw deal each time they are involved in accidents with other drivers. Ask many cab drivers and their response would be in the affirmative for a lot of them especially the crazy cabbies.

Getting a moving violation tickets from the cops are a common occurrence with many cabbies especially the crazy cabbies. And if you take a peep into their driving records you would see a long list of moving violation convictions. Through my 17 years as a Chicago cabbie I had just a few stops by cops and in a few of those I was summarily pardoned by the cop. One of them happened at O'Hare airport. I had just dropped a fare and was driving out from the drop off lane to join the through lane, when I saw the police blue flashing light behind me. I pulled over expecting the car to pass, thinking that he was on emergency call. But he stopped behind me. The cop stepped out and stood beside me and asked if I knew why he pulled me over. I honestly said no because I did not think I had committed any violation.

Then he said I did not use my turning light before joining the traffic. I told him that I thought I did and that I always did as a regular practice. He asked to see my drivers license. While I was fumbling with my wallet to bring out my license, I pleaded with to forgive me. I also told him that I have had clean driving record as a testament that I am a good driver. He took my license anyway and went back to his car. He came back and handed my license back to me and said: 'I have forgiven you; be careful next time.'

I thanked him and drove to the cab staging area at O'Hare. There I checked my cab over and discovered that the left rear turning light bulb was dead. So that was why I felt I did turn on my turning light and it appeared like I did not because the bulb was dead. However, I thanked God for sparing me from being charged for that because that would have attracted a heavier penalty for operating an unsafe vehicle.

The other time I was summarily pardoned was at

west Wacker Drive, in the front of Renaissance Hotel. Before the reconstruction of Wacker Drive there used to be a gap in the median in front of the hotel where drivers can enter or exit the hotel from or to the opposite lanes. But after the reconstruction, may be by act of omission the gap was closed, and the hotel management did not protest. So drivers entering from the opposite lane or exiting to the opposite lane must have to drive over the 3 inches high concrete median. So this night I was making exit from the hotel and going west of Wacker Drive.

I had to drive over the median. A police car pulled me over. The cop, a young lady stood beside my door and asked me if I knew that it was illegal for me to drive over the median. I told her that I did not know that. She took my license and after a long while came back and gave my license back to me and said I could go. What I figured out was that she might have been a rookie officer because she looked very young. She might have been informed by her senior partner or from the office that I did not commit the moving violation offense for which she pulled me over.

On one other occasion I received a ticket, it was as if the cop, if left with him, would not have given me the ticket. This was after I had explained to him that I honestly did not know that there was a stop sign at that intersection because a delivery truck was parked directly at the corner of the intersection making it hard for anyone who was not used to driving on that road to know that there was a stop sign there, And moreover it was in the night. He agreed with me, but said that that was not an excuse. However, he sympathized with me, and all the same handed the ticket to me and wished me good luck at the court.

Cabbies used to complain about being often 'harassed' by cops when discharging or picking up fares on Michigan Ave. and State Street. Usually when a cabbie runs the streets, he watches the entrance doors of offices or stores as fares exit from them to hail for cabs. If a cabbie stops to pick up especially on Michigan Ave and State Street and there is a cop nearby, he might pull the cab over and issue a ticket for obstruction of traffic violation. These kind of tickets are often dismissed at the courts because cabbies invoke the relevant city ordinances that allow cabbies to pick up and drop off at any time on these roads.

There are about 3 cops who are well known to cabbies and who seem to be assigned with the responsibility of ticketing errant cabbies in the downtown Chicago. Many times they disguise their presence by riding in an unmarked police car. Some of their special locations to catch cabbies are at cab stands at the hotels and on Wacker Drive.

They ticket cabbies for over loading of cab stands.

Another complaint of the cabbies against cops is what some cabbies call 'double ticketing.' The practice happens thus: a cabbie is pulled over for a particular violation offense. The cop informs him of his offense, collects his license and goes back to his car to write the ticket. When the cop returns to the cab driver and hands him the ticket a close look at the ticket will reveal that a second offense has been tagged in. Usually the tagged in offense is the seat belt violation, even though the cabbie has his belt fastened on before he was pulled over. The cabbies might protest, but the ticket is never rewritten.

Cabbies are quite a familiar customers at the City's traffic courts. The courts used to be located on LaSalle Street by the Chicago River north and was always a beehive of activities every day. Cabbies regularly make a good percentage of drivers making court appearances. There were usually a good number of traffic attorneys milling around looking for clients, especially cabbies, to represent.

The attorneys have their rooms from where they consult with potential clients. There were no protocols; all you need to do if you require the attorney's representation was to pay 30 or 35 dollars. Give the attorney your hearing room number, your ticket and time of hearing. You do not need to have known your attorney before letting him represent you at the hearing. Many times you may have just met the attorney for the first time on that day of hearing. The attorneys were sometimes overloaded with the number of cases they have signed up that oftentimes they get confused as they shuttle between one court room to the other. One or two times they confuse the ticket of one client with another.

Other times one could see them trying to appear on two cases at the same time. All in all cabbies get their money's worth from the traffic court attorneys. Most times they get cabbies tickets dismissed or procure for them supervision. If they are found guilty, which did not happen often, they get fined.

The attorneys do a good job on behalf of cabbies at the traffic courts. They understand the mentality of cabbies concerning time. So they make the hearing go fast. I am not familiar with what goes on at the Daley Plaza home of the traffic courts now because since they moved to Daley center from the Lasalle Street location, I have been there for one or two times.

When I review my 17 years experience as a cabbie, I cannot but thank the Almighty God for protecting and helping me drive safely on the roads and streets of Chicago. I am proud of my driving records.

My driving records as of today remains clean of any driving violation convictions. Six times I was hit by other careless drivers including twice by fellow cabbies. One time I was nearly fatally hit head on by a fleeing driver chased by the cops. Only a split seconds decision to turn my steering slightly to the right saved me from taking a direct hit from that car. My cab was totaled, but I escaped with no scratches on me. The driver directly behind me was taken away in a stretcher by an ambulance.

Chapter 7

CITY OF CHICAGO AND IT'S CABBIES.

The city of Chicago owns the sole authority to issue license or medallion to cab operators in the city metropolis. The medallion is usually auctioned within the range of the market price for the medallion and it usually open to the public. It is the medallion that gives the taxi operator the right to operate cab or cabs depending on the number of medallion the operator has.

The city also through the Department of Business Affairs and Consumer Protection (formally the Department of Consumer Services) regulates the operation of the cab industry in Chicago. It has in place rules, regulations and ordinances that are aimed at protecting the cab riding members of the public, the drivers and cab companies and individual owners. It fixes cab rate and monitors taximeter two times in a year. Taximeters used by city cabs are always sealed by the city to prevent unauthorized tampering. So all taxis in Chicago, operate meters that read the same rate at any time.

Chicagoans can be rest assured that it is almost impossible for the meters to be tampered with.

Some passengers, however, think that some meters are faster than others. In fact some of my passengers had on several occasions queried me on why my meter seemed to be running too fast. I always take time to explain to them the mechanism of the operation of the meter, to alley their suspicion.

The meter is calibrated on time and distance. If for instance, the meter is on and the cab is stationary, the meter continues to run at 20 cents for every 36 seconds. If the cab is running, the distance and time are both in operation. The meter changes by 2o cents either at 36 seconds or at 200 yards, whichever comes first. So if the cab is running on the highway the meter changes according to the speed the car covers a block or 200 yards. That is the reason why when the cab is running on the highway or the express, the meter increases swiftly and slowly when the cab runs on streets.

The city's regulatory authority also determines the type of cars that are permitted to be used as cabs in Chicago. They require that cars not on the approved list be retired after four model years. While cars from the approved list be retired after five model years. Also wheelchair Accessible Cars and Hybrid cars are allowed to be in service for six years. So cab riders should feel good about this because only new and road worthy vehicles are allowed to be used as cabs in Chicago. And not only that, these cab are subjected to a very rigorous mechanical, electrical and body inspections two times in a year by the city. So I can say without equivocation that Chicago cabs are more road worthy than most cars operating on Chicago roads and streets.

The city has elaborate rules, regulations and ordinances that govern cab operations of both drivers and owners. Some of those rules and regulations are not always agreeable to drivers and owners alike. Take for instance, the drug test requirement that was imposed on all drivers applying for chauffeur's license renewal.

This rule as far as I am concerned, is nothing but an insult on all the over 95% of responsible, family oriented and religiously cultured cabbies who make up the community of cab drivers in Chicago. It's a shame that the current administration seem to have no regard or respect for the cabbies' community. The previous administration of Commissioner Norma I. Reyes imposed the mandatory drug test only on drivers with one or more violations during the renewal year. The city will do well to reverse this draconian rule to show that it really respect the men and women of the cab drivers community.

The four model years limit to certain vehicles used as cabs is economically severe on cab owners. Five model years limit for all cars used for cabs in Chicago to me, seems quite appropriate, considering the present economic climate in the country. If the city really cares about the economic concern and well being of cab owners, especially the individual owners, the city could make it five model years or 200,000 miles, whichever comes later and as long as the cars pass the inspections This will surely benefit the individual owners who many times retire cars that have under 150,000 miles on them.

The mandatory imposition on cab drivers to accept credit cards as a means of payment for all cab rides is really unfair to cabbies. This is because this rule affects the take home profit of cabbies. Every ride that is paid with credit card amounts to 5% loss to the cabbie.

Since the city imposed this rule on cabbies, it could have been reasonable if the city had provided a free clearing house where cabbies can cash their credit cards receipts.

Imagine a cabbie grossing about $10,000 a year on a credit card transactions; that is a $500 loss to the cabbie for providing services to the public. This is not fair. The city could lighten the burden of this rule by enforcing a minimum of $10 for credit card payments by passengers. It should also be noted that some unscrupulous passengers have begun to abuse this use by deliberately carrying dud cards which are all declined by the machine. And the passenger would claim that he has no cash with which to pay.

In every cab there is usually a Rate Card which informs the passenger among other things, his rights, and the driver's rights. But the one some passengers, from my experience, tend to abuse is the passenger's right to, 'Have heat or air conditioning turned on or off at your request.' I think this right could be modified to read thus: 'You have the right to have the heat or air conditioning turned on or off at your request provided the outside temperature is 65 degrees for heat and 75 degree for air conditioning.'

I gave a ride to one young man on one beautiful fall afternoon. That afternoon the general temperature was around 70 degrees, but at the lake front it was below 70 degrees. I had all the front windows of my cab rolled half way down when I picked up this young man on Ohio Street. He was going to Belmont and Broadway. While we were on Lake Shore Drive heading north, he called my attention and requested that I turn on the A/C. I was surprised by the request, so I politely asked him if he had heath issues because the demand was unreasonable at the current temperature.

He admitted he was okay, but needed to have me turn on the A/C because it was his right as stated by the bill of right in front of him at the back seat. I told him that it was true that he had right, but I would decline to grant him that because he was making an unreasonable request. I told him that I would not put on the A/C at 60 something degrees because I had my own health to protect,. and that if he insisted, then he might have to take another cab. He told me to move on.

Another rule the city imposed on cabbies which they did not have enough clout to resist was the 'one call a day' rule. This rule mandates cabbies to fill one radio dispatch call per day from the so called under served areas of Chicago, particularly the far south and west sides of Chicago. Cabbies could not fight this rule because renewal of chauffeur's license was tied to the compliance of this rule.

The city had no choice but enact this rule when cab

drivers began refusing fares going to some dangerous neighborhoods in the far south and west sides of Chicago. Cab drivers refused service to these areas, particularly in the nights and if the passengers were young black males. We can recall that in the early nineties till around 1998, many cab drivers were incessantly robbed and many times killed by the passengers they picked up from downtown to these areas. I remember in 1996, I think, about 6 cabbies were robbed and murdered in Chicago.

The city first introduced the bullet proof shield partition between the driver and the passenger to protect cabbies from attacks. but that brought its own problems of discomfort to both driver and passenger. For the driver, it gives little leg room to stretch his legs, especially the tall drivers and when the A/C is on it makes the driver's section too cold for comfort. For the passenger, there is little leg room also, and when the A/C is on barely gets enough for comfort. Also the normal driver and passenger interaction is limited.

The city lately introduced the camera system which gave cabbies a choice between having a shield or a camera. Many drivers are opting for the camera and it appears like the shield is fading away. But for me, I preferred the shield to the camera because the shield actually prevents the attack while the camera mainly helps in the apprehension of the culprits after they might have done their dastardly deed. It is pertinent to say that since the introduction of these safety measures by the city the number of cabbies killed in the line of duty has drastically fallen. All the same, there are still some cab drivers who are afraid to take fares to those dangerous neighborhoods in the night.

A rule enforcement which the city took to the extreme was the issuance of what the cab drivers called 'Fly By Ticket' which is issued to cabbies purportedly found by the Traffic Aids standing, waiting or parking on any street in the Loop. These tickets are issued without the knowledge of the cabbie involved. The traffic aids who were manning every intersection and most street corners of Chicago Loop were the instrument of enforcement of the no standing, waiting or parking rule.

So whenever a cabbie stops to discharge or pick up a fare, the traffic aid, who may be about 50 yards away from the spot and may have no idea what the cab is actually doing there. Still he will go ahead and write the number and color of the cab and then later the address where the violation occurred. All these are written on a scrap paper and at the close of day transferred into the tickets. The ticket information is then sent to the cab company or the affiliation that would then supply the name of the cabbie and then the ticket is finally delivered to the cabbie.

Mayor Daley had so many of these traffic aids all over downtown and it appeared like their main assignment was to write fly by tickets to cab drivers for added revenue for the city. The issuance of these tickets became so rampant that some cabbies were sometimes receiving about three tickets a day. But cabbies fought these tickets vigorously by going for hearing at 400 West Superior Street Administrative Court. Some cabbies preferred to pay the 30 dollars penalty than spending their time attending the hearing. Most cabbies who go for the hearing win their cases because they always claim that they were either discharging or picking up fares when the ticket was written.

One of the conspiracy theories of the cabbies was that Mayor Daley employed all those traffic aids as rewards to his political supporters, but could not find money to pay their salaries. He then introduced the strict enforcement of the no standing, waiting or parking rule when they are aware that cabbies are exempted from this rule when they are on the act of discharging or picking up a fare.

The City of Chicago has not treated it's cabbies well. It does not seem to care much about cabbies interest and welfare in the city. The city seems only interested in collecting its taxes from the cabbies and cab owners without providing any services that benefit the cabbies. It now costs 600 dollars to renew a medallion; 936 dollars a year for Ground Transportation Tax for each medallion and other numerous taxes and fees.

The likely reason why cabbies are treated in this manner by the politicians is that there is no political consequence to pay because even though there are over 15,000 licensed cabbies in Chicago, they are not a strong voting block. Many cabbies live outside Chicago metropolis. Secondly, Cabbies do not have a united functioning union. So if Chicago cabbies were a united work group and all of them live within the City of Chicago, they could be capable of constituting a strong voting block that could no doubt attract the attention of Chicago politician who might begin to change their attitude towards cabbies and address their concern and interests.

The city is notorious for treating matters affecting cab drivers with levity. When cabbies demand for a legitimate fare increase, the city politicians often are not moved even when cabbies threaten a strike. Rather the city politicians will attempt to get the cab riding public against the cab drivers by making them think that cabbies demands were borne out of greed and not out of a legitimate economic situation. Some time they dare the cabbies to go on strike, knowing full well that cabbies are not united enough to carry out an effective strike.

Even when they agree to a fare increase, they do it grudgingly and try to tie it to some unrelated demands on cabbies. So a cab increase that needed purely economic consideration to pass, will have some social appendages attached to it by the city.

The city has never for once initiated any project that was directed towards the welfare of cabbies. For instance, the city arbitrarily increased the medallion renewal fees from 500 dollars to 600 dollars. Not only that, the city mandated that 50% of medallion owners to pay one extra year in advance because of the city's plan to enforce a two year renewal requirement beginning from 2014. They explained that the increase in renewal fees was to apply the extra 100 dollars from the increase as deposit into the Wheelchair Accessible Cab loan fund. In other words, the city is taxing the cab industry----the owners and the drivers-----to fund a city's program for the disables. If the city can tax the cab industry in order to provide a service for the disables in Chicago, Why can't the city tax the cab owners and drivers to provide some needed services for the cabbies in Chicago.

Public restrooms in downtown have been a serious need for cabbies since all the cab companies' offices relocated out of the downtown area. Cabbies could do with a public restroom in downtown. Union Station used to have a drive through restroom for cabbies at the lower level of the cab stand. This ceased to be after the September 11th,2001 terrorist attack on New York. This lower level cab stand and restroom at the union station was closed for purely security reasons.

Since then cabbies have had difficulties finding a place to answer nature's call while working within the city. Sometimes the hotels, which were the alternative place to go, shut their doors against cabbies. So drivers under pressure to empty their bladder, apply some unconventional methods to do so. It is no secret that many cab drivers especially the older ones have urinary containers or wide mouth bottles under their seats to do their business when pressed. It should be understood that about 60% of these drivers are 45 years to 60 years of age and sure do have the problems of aging and enlarged prostate. Some of which are frequency and urgency in urination. Some other cabbies, when stressed and pressed to go, just use discarded plastic cups from fast food restaurants to do their stuff and when they are done, dump the waste on the streets.

The lack of public restroom where cabbies could use while working in downtown is a very serious issue with cabbies. And the city could help solve this need if it really cares.

The argument that it is not the responsibility of the city to provide services to independent contractors, as cabbies are often referred to, and that it is the responsibility of the cabbies to take care of their needs. This does not sound realistic. The cabbies are not only paying their due taxes, but they are one of the unheralded ambassadors of the city of Chicago who have contributed not a little to the promotion of tourism in the city.

So the city politicians could do well to acknowledge this by providing drive through restroom facilities exclusively for the cabbies in downtown Chicago.

If the city would claim that it does not have the finances to execute such project, it could impose some taxes on cabbies just like it did for the Wheelchair Accessible taxicab loan fund. Cabbies might be willing to make a little more sacrifice in order to get the project done. The city could also improve the cabbies common room at O'Hare airport by reconstructing and improving the existing structure. The current building is nothing but an oven. The air conditioning units even when turned on to the maximum usually do not make it a comfortable place to stay during the hot summer months. The Midway airport does not even have any common room for cabbies.

Chapter 8

CHICAGO PEDESTRIANS, CYCLISTS AND CTA BUS DRIVERS---PURE ROAD HAZARDS

I actually rejoiced and celebrated the last night I returned from work and realized that I was not going to work the next day. I am retired! I rejoiced because after 17 years,6 months and 16 days as a cabbie on Chicago roads, I never hit a pedestrian or the dare devil messenger cyclist and was never seriously hit by the Big Bully of Chicago roads, CTA buses.

The first impression any motorist who drives regularly on Chicago downtown roads would have about Chicago pedestrians and bicyclists is their reckless disregard to traffic rules and their own safety on the road. Many times they act like zombies who could never be fatally wounded even if they are hit by an eighteen wheeler truck. Or like the fairy tale witchdoctor who has spare life tucked in his wardrobe so that if he is fatally hit, goes home and picks up the spare life in his wardrobe. Who can imagine a normal human being walking across a busy road or street without even taking a precautionary look at both directions of the road to ensure that he does not put his life in harm's way. For goodness sake, have vehicles lost the moving force to hit and kill any living thing on their paths? Or have modern technologies softened the force of vehicles to run over or hit and kill? If you are a regular driver on downtown streets you must have noticed that Chicago pedestrians are not scared of moving vehicles.

Time was in the days gone by when human beings were scared of moving vehicles and we were taught early in school the safe ways to cross the streets so as not to get hit or run over. These days it appears that nobody is taught anymore about pedestrian's responsibility in ensuring their safety on the roads they share with vehicles. That's why these days you find kids playing basketball in the streets and would not make way for the oncoming vehicle even when prompted to do so. Sometimes children run across busy streets without stopping first to see if it is safe to do so. Many times this has resulted in many fatal accidents. Often too, you see grown men and women saunter across a busy street as if they are in their living or family rooms. Some others are so engrossed with their phones, either texting or on call and are oblivious of their surrounding and it is only when they hear the horn that they are jolted into reality. So this is endemic to the entire population not just the children.

Driving daily on Chicago downtown roads is really a driver's nightmare and needs a load of patience and grace to overcome the menace of pedestrians on the road. For instance, the traffic lights are made for both motorists and the pedestrians and compliance to the lights helps to keep vehicular traffic flowing as well as protect the pedestrians from accidents. But what do you find in Chicago? The pedestrians do not obey the traffic lights. They walk across the intersections on green and willfully leave the responsibility of preventing an accident solely on the drivers. They do not differentiate between "walk" and "don't walk". They respond to the two the same way.

And as such they begin walking when the light shows "walk" and continues to walk when it shows "don't walk", and by so doing, turning cars are stranded in the middle of the road waiting for the pedestrians to complete their walk. Many occasions this happens under the nose of the cops or the traffic aids. To be honest, many times the cops and the traffic aids shout themselves hoarse trying to stop them. If by any chance a driver tries to make a turn at the intersection while the "walk" sign is on and the pedestrian is present, they would almost want to step in front of the moving car in an effort to claim their right. And if the driver is able to make the turn before the pedestrian gets in front, they will resort to hitting the trunk of the car or kick the rear tire.

I remember one day I was making a turn on south Wacker Drive and the pedestrian was about 3 steps short of stepping into the intersection. When he saw that I was turning, he quickened his steps, but I beat him to it. So he first of all hit my trunk and then kicked my left rear tire. "Well played," I mocked him as I noticed that he was walking with a slight limp. He must have hurt his toes.

Whoever made the pedestrians believe that they have more right to the use of the roads than the vehicles for whom the roads were specifically constructed? And that may be the reason why they cross the roads when fast moving vehicles are driving past and they make no effort to run across, but instead take their time to stroll across and expect the vehicles to stop for them. And if the driver honks at them, they throw a disdainful look at the driver as if to say: "How dare you honk at me when I am crossing the road?"

How can a person be so dumb at this day and time that there are lots of distracted drivers everywhere. There are those driving under the influence of alcohol and drugs. There are others, perhaps the majority of drivers, who are driving while distracted by electronic devices (DWDED) chiefs of them being texting, playing games, and talking on the phone (whether hand held or hand free, they make the same amount of distraction). In the prevalence of these drivers on our roads, one would expect that some pedestrians would be more cautious as they walk on roads. It is foolhardiness, in the present distracted driving milieu, for one to entrust the safety of one's life to an unknown driver and expect that he has noticed one as one walks across the road. Instead any wise pedestrian should be wary and highly alert when walking on the roads. Streets and roads that are used by motorists are not the place to go and claim your right. You may have your right, and as they say, be dead right.

The traffic laws are explicit and abundantly clear to all road users what their responsibility toward safety and order on the roads are. Every road user without exception is required to comply with all traffic laws to avoid lawlessness on the road. It will not work if all of the road users obey the rules and just one road user does not. For instance, if motorists comply with the laws and pedestrians violate them, the consequence will be an accident and vice versa. For example, "the law requires a driver to give the right of way to a pedestrian when the pedestrian is walking with a green light to a walking person symbol or to a "walk" signal. In Chicago, this is the one rule that pedestrian violate with impunity. Drivers will yield to them as they start walking across the intersection with green light to walk signal or walking person symbol", but would continue to walk when the signal shows "don't walk", and many times during the rush hours will have cars stranded in the middle of the intersection causing a backup of cars waiting to make a turn. This has become an acute problem during the afternoon rush hours, when workers are trooping to the train stations on foot. Cab drivers are usually the main victims of the traffic light disobedience by pedestrians. Many times cab passengers going to Union stations on Adams street and Oglvie train station on Madison would voluntarily drop off on Wacker Drive because of the long backup of cars waiting to turn west on Madison and Adams streets.

The "Illinois Rules of the Road" makes it clear that "drivers and pedestrians are both responsible for traffic safety" and the following are the laws that require a pedestrian to give right of way to a driver.

(1) "Pedestrians must yield the right of way to drivers by obeying traffic signals, observing walk lights and using crosswalk"
(2) "When crossing at any place other than a marked or unmarked crosswalk, pedestrian must give the right of way to drivers"
(3) Pedestrians must not run or walk into the path of a moving vehicle."

Some months ago I was on Randolph going west. As I approached State Street, the sound of an ambulance siren went off from behind so all vehicles stopped or pulled over to the left or the right to make way for the ambulance. Just as the ambulance got closer, a young man strolled out leisurely into the road and seemed to be oblivious of the presence of the ambulance or the sound of the sirens. The ambulance stopped for the young man and waited until he had strolled across.

The traffic laws are explicit about the rights and responsibilities of both the drivers and the other users especially the pedestrians. But it appears the Chicago traffic laws enforcers are one sided in the enforcement. They make it look like only the drivers should be responsible for the safety on the road while the laws placed it on both drivers and pedestrians. And that is why they are always going after drivers especially cabbies and issuing tickets for not yielding to pedestrians when in actuality it is the pedestrians who are crossing the road illegally.

Early 2013, the Chicago police department conducted undercover operation at some of the intersections in Chicago purposely to catch drivers who were not yielding to pedestrians at the crosswalks. The operation did not focus on pedestrians who were the chief culprits violating the crosswalk laws. The results of their operations were not publicly disclosed, but I bet you that they must have discovered that the pedestrians were more likely than drivers to violate the use of the crosswalk and the 'walk' and 'don't walk' lights.

It looks to me like the Chicago city authorities do not want to face reality that the pedestrians are to blame for most of the crashes involving drivers and pedestrians at crosswalks. According to Chicago Department of Transportation (CDOT) there are an average of 3000 crashes involving drivers and pedestrians leading to 50 fatalities every year in Chicago. 53% of all these crashes were recorded as intersections related and the most common pedestrian action at the time of crash was "crossing with signal". Another important finding by the CDOT was that 52% of the crashes that occurred within a signalized intersection involved a turning vehicle. Added to this finding by CDOT was that 3pm-6pm (the afternoon rush hours) recorded the highest number of crashes.

From my seventeen and half years of driving experience on Chicago roads I can submit that the city authorities can devise ways of checking the excesses of the pedestrians violation of traffic lights rules particularly the crosswalk signals. If they are really determined to reduce the incidences of pedestrians and driver crashes at the intersections, they should first begin with road crossing safety awareness education for pedestrians. Secondly, cops could be detailed to all busy intersections in downtown during the rush hours to control the unruly pedestrians and issue tickets to drivers who violate the crosswalk signals. Cab drivers would always be singled out as the likely main culprits whenever pedestrian—driver crashes are discussed. But CDOT findings found out the contrary. Taxi cab involvement in pedestrian crashes in downtown Central Business District was only 28%. This is quite low considering the fact that cabs make up about half of all vehicles plying the roads of downtown CBD. Outside the downtown Central Business District crashes involving cabs was a paltry 2%.

Another road hazard or menace every regular driver on Chicago downtown roads must endure or avoid are the daredevil messenger cyclists. I personally call them "death seekers" because of their reckless disregard to their safety as they go about with their business in downtown. They have no regard for traffic lights and road safety. They literally fly through intersections whether the light is green or red. I have personally witnessed near fatal crashes between these dare devils and drivers and on each occasion it was the cyclist that was, in my opinion, in violation. I have on two occasions missed crushing a cyclist who attempted to "fly" through the intersection while I had the green light. Only my alertness saved the cyclists from serious injuries or death. The sad fact of the matter is that Chicago authorities are aware of the unsafe riding habits of messenger cyclists on Chicago roads, but they have almost done nothing to rein in these crazy cyclists. Whenever accidents occur between cyclists and drivers, the news would be reported in a manner that would suggest that the driver might be the one at fault. In spite of the craziness of the messenger cyclists on the road, I have never heard or seen Chicago cops issuing tickets to cyclists. Rather the city rewarded them by reconfiguring downtown lanes in order to create lanes for cyclists. Not only that, the city created traffic lights for cyclists and as such cut drastically the time the lights allowed drivers to make turns. In fact the green lights for turning cars are about one third of the time the light for cyclists stays green. And most of the time there are usually no cyclist around. The consequence of the traffic light change is that it has created traffic slow down on most streets in downtown during the afternoon rush hour.

Long stretches of cars would be seen waiting to make turns while the bicycle lane light is green and with no cyclists around.

Come to think of it, for all the favorable attention or treatment the cyclists are getting from the city at the expense of the drivers, one would like to know if bicyclists pay any form of tax to use the road or share the road with drivers. Was the roads not built primarily for the use of vehicles? Any other users of the road, for example, the cyclists, could be accommodated, but not usurp more right than the primary users of the road. Since the configuration of lanes to accommodate the bicycle lane, the messenger cyclists have become even more brazen in their behavior on the road. Once they are on their lane they don't respect the presence of even the pedestrians or drivers who may be discharging passengers.

This chapter cannot end without my introducing to you the acclaimed dangerous hazard of Chicago roads. Ladies and gentlemen, please welcome the Big Bully of Chicago roads, the CTA bus drivers. What can I say. If you do not driver regularly in downtown you will not understand what I am saying. The CTA bus drivers are pure hazard on Chicago roads. Their employers make and enforce the laws so they are never ticketed for any form of dangerous driving or violation. They run red lights at busy intersections and seldom stop at stop signs. They swing into and out of traffic cutting off cars without consideration of the safety of those smaller vehicles. The Department of Business Affairs and Consumer Protection requires that cab drivers take the drug test every year before renewal of their chauffeur license.

I want to propose that CTA drivers undergo drug test every month to ensure that they are not sometimes driving under the influence of something.

I have had close brushes with CTA buses, but most of the time my defensive during style had saved me from what could have been accidents. But on one occasion I was not too fortunate. I was going north on the State street on the outer lane. In front of me was a CTA bus-- standing in a bus stop on the curb side lane. Just as I got to the middle of the bus, suddenly the bus swung out into my lane, cutting me off. The bus body was so close to me that there was no way for me to move forward without the bus damaging the right side of my cab. So I swerved my car to the left and stopped to avoid the tail end of the bus from making contact with my cab. But because there were cars on the right lane in front of the bus, the driver could not avoid making contact with the right side of the cab. The tail end of the bus brushed my right rear view mirror and knocked it out. The driver never stopped, so I drove past him immediately, stopped just in his front and confronted him. I asked him if he did not know that he hit me and damaged my car. He denied hitting me. I had already called 911 and the police arrived. After the police had looked at the my cab and the bus and heard from us how the accident happened, he went to the bus driver and told him in low tones that he was at fault.

Meanwhile a CTA officer had arrived and accessed the accident and the damage to my car then advised me to file claims with the CTA.

Chapter 9

ODD AND WEIRD PASSENGERS

A lot of folktales have been told about taxi drivers and ghost passenger. How cabbies have inadvertently picked up and given rides to ghost passengers. By the nature of their work and responsibility, cab drivers are required to pick up any passenger who demands a ride. There are no restrictions about who they pick up on their daily drives as cabbies.

There was even a day a dirty, mentally sick and homeless man jumped into my cab while I was waiting at the light. I was prepared to give him a ride if he was coherent enough to say where he wanted to go. However, he really did not have anywhere to go, but was just playing pranks. He quickly left my cab at the next stop sign leaving behind a thick whiff of the most stinking odor that has ever hit my nose. This odor was so thick and nasty that it stuck in my nostrils and the entire cab.

I had to stop and clean the back seat with the wind shield wiper fluid and spray air refresher in the cab before I could continue work.

There is this story I heard from fellow cabbies when I was a rookie driver many years ago. It was a story about a young rookie cabbie fresh from Africa who had never heard or witnessed a Halloween celebration. On one halloween night at about 11.30 pm he picked up a male halloween celebrant at Halsted and Armitage streets, who was going to Irving Park and Southport. The passenger didn't seem to have any costume on. The cabbie who was doing the night shift took the LSD to Irving Park and west on Irving Park.

As they drove along, he and his passenger never spoke to each other. They passed Sheridan Road and headed towards Clark Street. As they approached the cemetery area on the south/east of Irving Park and Clark he began observing some different small groups of people in flowing black dresses sauntering along and across the road like ghosts and zombies. He slowed down as his heart beat began to race. He could not understand what to make of what he was seeing. He began to accelerate in order to leave the cemetery area quickly. Back home as a child he had often been told that ghosts sometime came out in the night from their graves to mingle with humans. Then suddenly he heard a deep throat and weird grunt from his back seat and quickly he took a look from his rear view mirror. He let out a throaty manly scream. By the aid of the faint street light he could see that his passenger had turned into a "devil" with a skeleton head covered with a black hood and with glowing orange light in the huge sockets of the skeleton's face. He let out another scream and was almost losing control of the car.

The passenger noticed that the driver was genuinely scared and could crash the cab if not stopped. He shouted at him to stop as he had removed the devil's head.

"Man, what's wrong with you?"He asked with a smile on his face,This is halloween;

I am not a ghost or the devil. I am a man like you."

When the cabbie realized his mistaken assumption, became embarrassed and apologized to his passenger and confessed that he had just come to America and had never witnessed a halloween celebration.

There was this black young man in his forties I picked up at south Michigan Avenue in downtown. He was very neatly dressed in a pair of beige pants and off white sport shirt He had an expressionless look. on his face,but clearly grim. He looked like somebody who was going to have a confrontation with somebody. When he had settled down in the backseat, I asked him for his destination.

"Oak Park" he said. We hit the Eisenhower express road. As we drove along my passenger requested that I turn up the volume of my radio that was playing some Christian music from my favorite Christian radio station. I was always tuned to this radio station when I want to listen to inspirational and edifying music. We continued our trip while the music played. As we approached our exit at Harlem, I looked at my passenger and noticed that he was sobbing. I offered him some tissue papers and asked what the matter was.

"I think the man up stair is talking to me."

"Good. Whatever He says to you do it.,I said to him and using his reference to God as the" man up stair", I added ; "He is a good man and cares about our good"

"I sure will," he assured me.

"Good for you."

We drove for a block and he instructed: "Hey cabbie, stop here, I don't need to continue with this trip." I could notice that his facial expression looked radiant and happy.

He looked like a person who has had some disturbing burden lifted. I imagined that whatever it was that he was going to do was not a pleasant one and may not have yielded a positive outcome. Before I drove off, he came to the front passenger door window and bent down to speak to me. He peered through the rolled down window and extended his hand for a hand shake. I took his hand and he gave me a firm grip and held it as he said: "Man, you're my angel; God has used you to stop me from the evil I was about to do."

"Praise the Lord!"I excitedly said as I squeezed his palm, let go his hand and drove off.

Still talking about odd passengers, I was driving past the bar situated on State street, between Hubbard and Kinzie streets, when I was flagged down by this man who came out from the bar. When I stopped in front of the bar, he told me to wait a minute as he went back into the bar to call the passenger. After a short while, I saw two men, one on each side of a man, who looked like he was in a drunken stupor,trying to prop him up to walk to my cab. At first I wanted to drive off because I did not want to deal with the man in such drunken state. But I mustered courage and waited. They brought him close to my cab. I asked the lead man who brought him into my cab," I hope you're going with him?"

"Oh yeah," he answered. But no sooner had he dumped him in my cab, handed me a twenty dollar bill and said : "drop him at Kinzie and Clinton," than he ran back to the bar. It was a weekend night.

I tried to communicate with this man, but not a word came out of him. He was dead drunk. I was really stuck. What do I do? I drove off not knowing exactly what I was going to do with this man when we arrive at Kinzie and Clinton. When I arrived at the intersection of Kinzie and Clinton I did not know which of the building was his. I came out of my cab and tried to wake the man up, but no response. It was like trying to move a log of wood. I tried shouting: "hey man, wake up and let's go." No response. Fortunately I saw a young man standing in the front of one of the buildings. I went to him and begged him to come see if he could identify the man I have in my cab. He excitedly joined me and immediately he took a look at him recognized him and yelled his name and shook him very hard until he stirred up and said some incoherent things.

Both of us helped to lift him up and dragged him out of the cab. The moment he came out of the cab, I left him to his friend and drove off. Little did I know that the man had urinated in my cab. I did not know until I picked up a party of three people who noticed it. They quickly jumped out of my cab. I could not work anymore. I drove to Yellow Cab garage at Elston Street to clean up. I arrived at Elston Street at about 1145pm. After cleaning my cab it became late to continue to work. So I closed for the day.

Since I have told about the drunk man, let me also tell about the "drunk" woman I gave a ride to Oak Park. It was another weekend and I was running the streets searching for fares. This time I was going east on Hubbard street. Hubbard, from Wabash street up to Wells is usually busy on the weekend because of the large number of bars and clubs there.

On State and Hubbard Streets three passengers, two men and a woman, flagged me down. I noticed that the woman, a white lady in her forties was sandwiched between the two men and as they began walking to my cab, I noticed also that the lady appeared to be staggering and unable to walk steadily. The first man opened the door to let the lady in and then shut the door. The other man was already walking away. The man who let the lady in came to my side and instructed me to take the lady to Oak Park and that she would give me her home address.

The time was about 11pm when I took off to Oak Park. As we got into the Eisenhower Express way, I asked her where I was going to make exit into Oak Park--- Austin or Harlem? She said Austin. Meanwhile she has been busy talking to herself at the back seat, using all manner of intimate sexual vulgarities. She was throwing the F word in every phrase she spoke. There was nothing in the book of lewdness that she left unspoken in her drunken soliloquy.

I exited at Austin and she instructed me to turn left to Roosevelt and right on Roosevelt.

After driving for about three quarters of a mile on Roosevelt she asked where we were. I told her that we were still on Roosevelt going west.

"Oh no! You're taking me to the wrong way you –F-word—driver. Go back to Austin, ass @#$@", she angrily cursed.

"Ma'am, I am only following your direction. You know that you have not given me the address of where I should drop you off," I responded as I pulled over out of frustration.

"Now may I know the address of your home? I will not move until you tell me."

"I have forgotten; I can't remember."

"You can't remember your own home address?"

"No," she replied.

"Okay, I'll call 911 for the cops to come and help me."

This seemed to have done the trick. She pleaded with me not to call the cops. She then proceeded to direct me again without giving me her home address or street name. I became very suspicious and cautious. I began to wonder if she was really drunk as she initially acted to be when she boarded my cab. Then I told her that I will give her just one more chance to give me true direction to her address or I call the cops for help.

This time she told me to head west again on Roosevelt. So I had to turn around and head west on Roosevelt and after about two blocks she told me to turn left. I did. Another left, and then a right.

"Stop!" she ordered.

I stopped.

"No, keep going," she instructed again. We drove for about half a block to a group of houses--- perhaps single family homes—on both sides of the street and with cars tightly parked on both sides of the street. The street was dimly lit and there were nobody in the street. My sixth sense was now fully activated and alert. As she asked me to stop again she also added that she would be going in to get money to pay me.

I promptly told her that she would need to leave her purse in the cab as she goes to get the money. She asked why and I said it was just to make sure that she comes back. She released another barrage of F—words curses at me and said she would not do that. By this time I became convinced that this lady was not really drunk as she initially acted to be, but had been acting up in order to cause some dispute so that she will find some excuse not to pay for her ride. I quickly came out of my cab and stood at the door as she alighted from the cab. I repeated to her that she would need to leave her purse in the cab as she goes to get her money. Again she swore that she will not. So I held on to her purse and she began hitting my hand. I held tightly to the purse and began shouting for help.

I could see several neighbors peeping out from their windows. She kept hitting me and demanding that I leave her purse. I kept defending myself while demanding for my money. Suddenly I noticed the flashing blue light of a cop car racing towards us. I did not call the cop though I was getting ready to call them. May be the neighbors did. When the cop arrived both of us still had our hands on the purse. The cop heard her as she continued to curse. The cop asked me first what was happening. I told him. By this time I had let go the purse. The cop asked her if she hit me. She acknowledged she hit me because I refused to let go her purse. Then the officer asked me how much the fare was. I showed him the meter which was 25 dollars and some cents He then asked the lady if she was ready to pay. She said she has money in her room. The cop followed her to her home which was about 3 houses from where she had asked me to drop her off.

This is what passengers who had planned to steal service normally do. They do not usually ask the cabbie to stop in front of their address. They rather make the cabbie stop somewhere close to their address so that it would be difficult to trace them after they had gone and not return.

After about 10 to 15 minutes of waiting the cop came back with my money and told me that a neighbor helped out. The cop was kind enough and even apologized on behalf of the lady.

One of the things I found interesting as a cabbie is the behavior of married middle aged women whenever their professional duties bring them to Chicago. When majority of them are in the cab together, they don't talk about their families or their marriages. Rather they talk excitedly about their college or their high school days experiences and escapades. You can almost see the glow on their faces as they retell their younger days experiences. When they are ready for party, they go together and enjoy together. They prefer the younger people's bars on State and Division as if they want to recapture the fun they might have missed because of marital responsibilities.

When they are slightly tipsy, the songs you hear them sing like teenage girls, are the 1970s and 1980s oldies.

For the men, they talk like young college guys. They poke fun on one another and talk excitedly about college days and their sexual lives. Apart from eating in the choice steak houses in the city, they also ask for the gentlemen's and strip clubs.

One Friday night at about 10 pm, I picked up a gentleman on State and Oak, close to the "Viagra Triangle". He could be in his early fifties. When he entered the cab, I noticed that he was furtively looking around as if to make sure he was not being followed. Then he softly spoke in a low tone of voice to ask me to take him to the nearest strip club. I told him the nearest was about 6 miles away. He requested that I take him there. On our way we drove in silence except for the Christian music songs coming from my favorite Christian music radio station that was playing. As we drove along I could hear him humming the tune of a popular Christian song that was playing on the radio. At the end of the song he called my attention and asked if I could turn around and take him to his hotel instead. I asked if he was aborting the trip and he said yes. I drove along to the next exit and headed back to downtown. As we headed back to his hotel he asked if I was a person of faith. I said yes.

"I believe God arranged that I ride in your cab," he

said. "You're really a good man and God has used you to stop me from being unfaithful. The spirit of lust was pushing hard on me to do this, but God stopped me through your Christian music before I could do it.

Thanks so much."

"You're welcome," I acknowledged, "It's no big deal; I am happy for you.

When we arrived at his hotel, he gave me a 100 dollars bill. As I reached into my pocket to give him his change, he said, "It's all yours; you deserve it."

I drove away feeling real good inside of me.

The next odd passenger incidence was a true account told me by the cabbie friend who was directly involved. He picked up this male passenger at the front of Midwest Stock Exchange on Van Buren Street. He was going to Irving Park and Lake Shore Drive As they drove along my cabbie friend noticed that his passenger was uneasy. He was talking to himself and at times would slap one of his thighs hard and mutter some curses at himself. Then as they joined the traffic on Lake Shore Drive from Jackson, he asked the cabbie : "Hey cabbie, would you like to make extra 20 bucks from this trip?'

The cabbie wondered what that could be. Could it be that he is trying to engage the cabbie into some illegal activity? The cabbie was cautious as he replied, "I would like to if it is something legal and something I can do"

"It is quite a simple thing to do to earn extra 20 bucks"

"Let me hear it, "the driver demanded.

"Now hear it; I lost a lot of money today at the trading and it was all my (f—word) stupid mistakes. I cannot forgive myself yet, but if you can accept to curse me out with all curses you know and do not know from now till you drop me off in the front of my residence. May be I could feel better and the 20 bucks will be yours. But be careful you that you keep my mum out of this, okay?"

The cabbie was not convinced that he meant what he said and was reluctant to proceed. "Come on man, curse me. Go ahead and curse me"

The cabbie now realizing that his passenger meant what he asked for began to curse him.

He ran out of curses so he began to create new ones and never ceased until they arrived in front of the passenger's residence. In addition to the meter price, he added the 20 dollars as he promised and thanked the cabbie for a job well done.

Chapter 10

CABBIES AND WOMEN OF EASY VIRTUE

A lot of tales have been told about cabbies and women of easy virtue. In every county of the world where taxi cab transportation is operated cab drivers have often been associated with women of easy virtue. I cannot explain why cabbies are attracted to these types of women. It could be, perhaps, because of the fact that cabbies carry cash most of the time. That was before now. These days cab drivers do not carry much cash any more. As of now, about half of a cabbie's daily service is paid with credit, debit cards and other forms of vouchers. But before now, cabbies were known to carry a lot cash on them. That may be the reason why these women prefer to make propositions to cabbies. From my own experience, it would take a cabbie with high integrity and principles to resist the temptation posed by these women.

I could still recall as if it was yesterday my encounter

with a young white woman in her late twenties or early thirties, who claimed she was a stripper. I had driven for about 2 years when this happened. I picked her up from the far north side. Wrigleyville area to be precise, at about 7pm and she asked to be dropped off at Wabash and Madison in downtown. It was a hot summer day and she wore a short sleeveless dress held by a pair of tiny strings to the shoulders. We drove in silence while on Lake Shore Drive, but she broke the silence as we got into the loop.

"Hey driver, I am a stripper"

"Excuse me", I pretended I did not understand what she had just said.

"I said I am a stripper--you know, I strip and dance before guys. I am also available if they need me. Look!"

I looked back from my rear view mirror and saw that she had exposed a pair of bare breast.

"What! Why are you doing that?." I yelled. She quickly covered up.

"That's my job and I am available if you need me. I stay at this hotel; ask for Ann."

We pulled over to the south west corner of Madison and Wabash and she paid me and included a very good tip.

"Wow! "Can I believe what has just happened?"I said to myself in disbelief as I drove off.

On another occasion, I picked up a middle aged white woman in front of a pub on south Wabash avenue. She looked reserved and responsible in appearance as she walked towards my car to board. She should be about 45 years old, and seemed to be in high spirit.

"Hey ma'am, how's your day going?" I asked her as she settled down in her seat.

"I am doing okay and how are you doing, too"

"I am good, thank you"

"Driver, I know your accent; you're from Nigeria, right?"

"Oh yes. How do you know that?" I asked

"I used to have a Nigerian boyfriend while in college. I had a boy with him, but he left me when the boy was a toddler and went back to his country. I miss him. He was real good in the bedroom..."

I did not like the angle this conversation was about to go, I thought. So I quickly tried to steer it to another direction before she could finish her sentence. I thought of the anticipated presidential election match up between President Bush and Senator John Kerry. "Who are you voting for, Bush or Kerry?"

" I am not a political person. I don't care who wins or loses. They both are the same. Don't trust politicians," She said.

"You're very right". I concurred.

"Driver, are you married?", she inquired.

"Yes I am. I have 4 kids. My oldest is 18 and my youngest is 11 years"

"Good for you"

"Thank you"

As we got closer to her destination at Lawrence and Broadway she got on her phone and was speaking to a female voice with such a raunchy expressions that would clear any lingering doubt about the type of woman she was. After a while on her phone she addressed me again.

"Driver, how late are you working tonight?"

"I am almost getting ready to close. You might even be my last fare," I replied. I usually close work on regular days at 8pm while on weekends I close at 12 midnight.

"Really, then you can't refuse an invitation to go have some beer on me."

"I'm sorry to disappoint you; I do not drink alcohol. Thanks for the invitation."

We came to a stop in front of the pub on Broadway and Lawrence. She brought out a 20 dollar bill and held it out and as I stretched my hand across the shield to take the bill. She grabbed my wrist and began gently squeezing my palm as she pleaded with me to go with her to the pub to have some drinks.

"Come on driver, one bottle will not harm you. Maybe we could spend the night together; I live close here."

I pulled my hand away. "Sorry ma'am, I am married and also I am a preacher. I do not engage in extramarital affairs"

"I am sorry, I did not know you're a preacher", she apologized.

"It's okay," I replied.

She paid and surprisingly added a good tip.

It was another beautiful spring Friday evening when I picked up a lady, I guess was in her early forties, dressed in a pair of tight fitting blue jeans and a shirt. She flagged me down in front of the restaurant located on State and Monroe. She entered the cab and announced that she was going to the far north side and requested that I go through La Salle street to lake shore drive. I asked her why she would want me to take La Salle instead of going direct from Monroe street. She said she wanted to enjoy the scenery as we drove along.

"This is my special day, driver". She announced.

"What makes it special," I asked.

"Today is my birthday!"

"Oh., good for you".

I then proceeded to sing to her the usual birthday song.

"Thank you driver; that was kind of you"

"You're welcome."

"Driver, can you do me a favor?"

"What is it?"

"Please let me sit in front with you". She requested

I knew it was against the rule to admit a fare to the front seat when the fare does not have any disability with legs or knees. Or besides not having three other passengers the fare has to have a medical report from a doctor recommending a front sit preference, but I thought I could humor her on her special day by breaking the rule.

"Eh--eh, Okay, you can come over". I stopped to let her in the front seat to sit beside me. We drove quietly to her residence on the far north side. When she had paid me she was slow in leaving the cab, like there was something on her mind she wanted to say. Finally with one leg out, she turned around facing me and said with a smile on her face,

"Driver,, would you like to come with me to my apartment and share some birthday cake and some wine with me? I mean it", she said.

"Oh, I am very sorry you can see I am still working. It's not possible. Thanks for the invitation".

She was visibly sad as she attempted again to leave. I did not feel any guilt for turning down her invitation. I have principles and I must maintain it. Finally she turned her face towards me, this time very close to my face with her lips tilted towards mine and said. "Okay, now give a birthday kiss." I turned my head back and held up my two hands between my face and hers to avoid her lips meeting mine if she were to try to kiss me.

"No. Please, I can't do that. I'm sorry I don't kiss strange women. Besides, I am a preacher and I'm married."

I could see she felt wounded and humiliated, but I couldn't help it. She dejectedly walked towards her residence as I drove off.

Another encounter with another woman happened on one October Friday night. Usually on Fridays I start work in the morning and close work at 12 in the night. The reason why I work late on Fridays was because Fridays being the beginning of the weekend,, usually had an extended night activities. So I usually take advantage of this to work longer hours so as to make more money. On this very day I had worked till it was closing time, so I began heading for home to the far south suburbs. Normally I go through south Michigan and join the Dan Ryan expressway through Cermak road to China town. The reason I take this route is because sometime I usually pick up fares going to south side. This was exactly what happened this very night. I was flagged down on south Michigan Avenue by a middle aged black lady who was dressed like she was returning from a party. She boarded my cab and announced her destination to far southeast side of Chicago. That was a long distance. We drove straight to 31st street and from there to Lake Shore Drive.

She told me how she had a good time at the party. How she had some good dancing time at the party. She even told me about the young lady who got offended because she caught her boyfriend or husband several times exchanging winks with her.

"Do you know that she walked up to my table and warned me to leave her man alone.. I did not initiate anything; It was all her man that began it all" she narrated to me.

"You know some men are never satisfied with one woman, even if they have miss universe as their woman. I hope the young lady did not initiate a confrontation with you" I interjected.

"No I would not have allowed that to happen. But do you know what happened afterward?"

"No", I replied.

"Her husband or boyfriend walked to my table and asked me for a dance. I got up and joined him to the floor and had a good dance with him. He slipped his card into my palm. I don't intend to call him".

" I support that you don't call him," I advised.

"He looks like a philanderer to me. He's already in a relationship; why should he be chasing you in the presence of his woman."

" I think you are right, driver."

We arrived at her residence a beautiful single family home. She paid me and added a very good tip.

"Well driver, I have had a very good night out, but do you know what? I am going to have a lonely night in my home tonight. Please do wait until I enter into my house".

"I am waiting". I assured her.

She walked a few steps towards her entry door, but hesitated and then turned and walked back to the cab. She bent slightly and stuck her head through the window and said softly.

"You're a good man and I can see that from the way you talked. You can park your cab in the driveway and come in let's have a good time together. I have some good wine; I am sure you'd enjoy them. Common". She said as she winked seductively at me.

"I am sorry my dear pretty lady. You can see that it's almost 1: am. My wife is waiting for me at home and she would be worried if I don't get home soon. Besides I don't drink alcoholic beverages. Thanks. It has been a pleasure giving you a ride".

I could see the disappointment on her face as she slowly turned and walked towards her entry door. I waited to see her step into her home.

"Have a good night, ma'am". I yelled and drove off.

These are just a snippet of the kind of temptations cab drivers face often with women. Some cabbies who have given way to these temptations have had their reputation tainted; robbed of all the money they made that day. Some others have even been accused of sexual assault. Cabbies be warned of these women of easy virtue.

Chapter 11

MY SHARE OF CELEBRITIES PATRONAGE

It is a known fact that cabbies do enjoy the patronage of social personalities and celebrities from the entertainment world, Hollywood, the sports world, Politicians and Political leaders. I really did have my own share of Celebrities patronage.

On this beautiful summer night I picked up a party of four young adult men who might be in their early twenties. I guessed they might even be college students. I picked them up at North Ave and Wells Street and they were going to Grant Park. There was some show going on in the Park that night. As they boarded my cab, I observed that the young men were in a light and jovial mood like they might have visited some bars.

As soon as they settled in their seats one of them from the back seat asked: "Hey Cabbie, have you ever given a ride to a Celebrity before?"

I was taken aback by this question because I did not have an answer. In short I did not know if I had ever given a ride to a celebrity within the one and half years I had driven cab in Chicago.

"I don't know; in short I can't tell if I have ever given a ride to a celebrity. Why do you ask?"

"Well, today you have a celebrity right here in your cab," a different voice from the back seat said. There were some chuckles of approval and support for that statement from the other two guys at the back seat.

"Really, "I said as I scanned their faces to try to guess which of them it might be. I observed that the guy in the front seat had not spoken a word since they entered my cab. He had been kind of reserved.

"Look at the face of the guy sitting beside you; know him?"

"No, I don't," I answered. However, I took a look all the same, but could not make out who he was. Moreover I considered him too young to be anybody important so I concluded that this must be some pranks.

"Could you please tell me who he is; I'm dying to know." I pleaded

"You're sitting beside the next mayor of Chicago"

"The next mayor of Chicago.?" I asked incredulously.

"Yes, you have the son of Mayor Richard Daley sitting beside you."

"Yeah yeah yeah," his companions yelled in approval.

He never said a word, but continued to grin. We exchanged friendly glances as we arrived at Monroe Street and Columbus---- their destination. He paid for the ride and added a huge tip.

On another occasion I was heading south on State Street and Division when a party of four burly men flagged me down. They were physically sturdy in built and they were either wearing full grown beards or some days old unshaven beards.

"Hyatt hotel" One of them announced.

Initially I could not make out who they were until they began making references to "last night" game and about some hits on players. I then recalled that the Chicago Hawks played the Detroit Red Wings the previous night at the United Center and lost.

I took a look at their faces to try to identify them, but I was not an ice hockey fan then because I was still trying to understand the game. I was used to field hockey which is majestic and beautiful to watch. Ice hockey in my opinion is a brutal and violent game that has degenerated into a cowboys style of fighting and racking with brutal hits and punches that are regarded as legal. So to confirm these guys were ice hockey players I watched out to see the characteristic missing teeth. Sure enough two of them had missing frontal teeth.

These were Detroit Red Wings players indeed. As we pulled into Hyatt Regency and as they were about leave my cab, I shouted "Go Red Wings!" Two of the guys turned, smiled and gave me a thumb up.

The NBA usually conducts a yearly pre-draft evaluation program at the Moody Bible Institute basketball court. Often during this time cabbies do often pick up young men with unusual heights. That's when we know that prospective NBA players, coaches managers and official are in town.

On one of such occasion, I picked up two older gentlemen perhaps in their sixties. One of them had a little boy of about 8 to 10 years of age tugging along with him. They boarded my cab and announced that I should take them to the Field Museum.

One of them requested that I allow him to sit in the front seat because of his knees. I obliged. When he had sat down I looked at him closely and discovered that the face was familiar. I began to rack my brain to remember who he was. I may not have seen the face live, but must have seen it on the t v screens or on the pages of the newspapers. The two men were talking about NBA basketball. Then suddenly I got it ! This is the mighty JERRY WEST the man whose image is on the logo of the NBA, a hall of famer, former General Manager of the Lakers-----the man who drafted Kobe Bryant.

"Yes!" I exclaimed, not minding that he was sitting beside me in the front.

"Sir, I think I know who you are."

"You do?" he asked softly.

"Yes, you are----"

His companion sitting in the back seat did not allow me the privilege of saying it myself.

"Jerry West," he interjected with a big grin on his face. "And this is his grandson", he added.

"Tell you what sir," I started," my son will never believe me if I tell him that you were sitting beside me in my cab today. So could you please sign for me on this diary to show my son as a proof that I met you today?"

He graciously obliged and signed. And asked if my son played basketball?. When I dropped them in the front of the Field Museum he shook my hand and thanked me.

On another occasion I had the privilege of picking up another celebrity. He was the incomparable Norman Van Lier, the ex Chicago Bulls star guard of yesteryears, and also a bull's TV analyst.

On this particular day I picked him up as I headed north on Michigan Ave. Initially I did not recognize that he was the one I had picked up because I did not look at the face of the man who entered my cab. But as I drove to his destination he picked up conversation with me. Immediately I recognized the voice. I looked back through my rear view mirror and recognized the face.

"Norman Van Lier." I exclaimed.

"I recognized your voice the moment you spoke. What a pleasure to give you a ride. I always enjoyed your analysis of the Bulls game on the TV. I love your no nonsense approach to the game. The guards you guarded during your playing days must have dreaded your presence on the court," I complimented him.

He just grinned and said: "You must be a fan of basketball and the Bulls."

"Yes as a Chicagoan you have no choice, but to love the Bulls, "I replied.

"Can the Bulls ever become dominant again?"

"You can never tell," he said," one or two good drafts can make a huge difference for a team that is struggling like the Bulls are right now."

"May God help our Bulls "I prayed.

"Amen to that." he responded.

A few months after this encounter with Norman, he passed away after a brief illness.

Richard Dick Gephardt was a well known former national leader of the Democratic party. On the very day I gave him a ride I picked him up at the Daley Plaza. He was going to the Union League Building on Jackson. I did not talk to him until we arrived at the front of the Union League Building.

"Sir, welcome to Chicago," I greeted him.

"Thank you."

"I hope you're enjoying your retirement."

""Yes, thanks.."

From the look on his face he was surprised that I recognized him and he will not encourage any conversation with me. He paid me and walked into the building.

My next celebrity was picked up at the O'Hare airport. I had picked up a party of 3--- two women and one man. The ladies were white while the man was a black. The man sat with me in the passenger seat in the front while the two ladies sat at the back seat. From the moment these passengers entered my cab I did not cease from looking at the older woman because I was trying to recollect who she was. I believe I had seen her face on the TV or on the pages of the newspapers.

We drove from O'Hare airport to downtown without my getting any hint from my memory who this woman was. I kept racking my head to get some hints and then it came. Could she be Mrs. Elizabeth Dole? I thought. She looked very much like her. I kept this to myself until we drove into downtown.

Then I leaned to the man sitting with me in the front and whispered: "This woman looks very much like Mrs. Dole."

"That's right; it's her," he replied.

"Yes!" I exclaimed under my breath in exhilaration.

This was Mrs. Elizabeth Dole, the United States Senator, the would have been first lady of America had her husband, Mr. Bob Dole, beaten Mr Bill Clinton in their Presidential election duel in 1996. Mrs. Dole was a very attractive lady even at her age.

The lady with her, I guessed must be her personal assistant and the man her security detail.

Chapter 12

THE BAD AND RECKLESS DRIVERS ON THE ROAD

If you make your living by driving any type of vehicle and you are on the road at least half of the day every work day of the week, your opinion and knowledge of all categories of drivers who use the road, particularly the bad and dangerous ones should be respected, right? After two decades of driving on Chicago roads both as ordinary Chicagoan and a cabbie, I have identified the reckless and dangerous drivers that consistently cause accidents on the roads.

The information you are going to receive from my knowledge and experience will certainly stir your desire for more defensive driving and as such reduce the possibility of your involvement in auto accidents on the road.

My first category of dangerous drivers on Chicago roads are the young ladies between the ages of 18-27 years. My first accident as a cabbie was a hit from behind by a 22 years old lady. In fact four out of the six times I have been involved in accident have been hits from behind by young ladies. On this very day I, was driving South on Wabash on a snowy day with some accumulation on the ground. I made a stop at a stop sign and the car directly following me, driven by this young lady, hit me. You would have thought that on a snowy day with some inches of accumulation that every driver would be cautious on the road. No speeding, give the car in front of you a safe distance and to be alert. But it was not so for this young lady.

She was following me very closely and seemed to be in a hurry and not particularly paying attention to the road. When I stopped at the stop sign, I momentarily took a look at her before she hit me and found that her face was turned to her left and so did not realize that I had stopped. Bang! She hit me! She was lucky because there was no damage to my cab and I let her go even though Yellow Cab Company demands that a driver must obtain a police report for any accident no matter how minor it was. I did not go to the Police because of my lease time it would consume.

I don't know if I am alone, but, I am convinced that young ladies are the most dangerous drivers on the roads of Chicago. They do not obey traffic rules and regulations. They often run red lights and do not usually stop at stop signs. What they do at stop sign is to slow down and go.

The young ladies are the opposite of their older counterparts who are more responsible and careful on the road. Unlike the older ladies these young ladies are notoriously careless and irresponsible on the road. They speed and are very aggressive on the road.

They force their way into the lanes of other motorists and dare them to hit them. It is not only these reckless and aggressive style of driving that typify the young ladies as dangerous drivers on the road, but the other dangerous habits they exhibit on the road.

One day on a busy downtown Chicago afternoon rush hour traffic, I saw a young lady driver holding the steering wheel with the last two fingers and the thumb of her left hand while the first two fingers held on to a lighted cigarette she was smoking.

With her right hand she held a lipstick she was applying on her lips. And she was applying her lipstick using the vanity mirror on her car's roof. This was really the multitasking ability of women in display. I marveled at the 'spectacle.' I am sure you would too.

Their other dangerous driving habit is the use of cellphone for talk and texting while driving. The young ladies are the most guilty of this. Two times I was hit from behind were by girls who were either texting or talking on the phone. In one of the accidents a young girl hit me from behind after I had stopped at the stop light. We both came out our cars after she had hit me. She came out still talking on her phone. I thought she was calling the police so I relaxed. Not until I overheard some of her conversations that I realized that she was still talking to her boyfriend and not to the police.

" I thought you called the police?" I asked her.

"No, I am still talking to my boyfriend." She boldly said without any remorse in her attitude.

When the police eventually came, she was still on the phone giggling unconcerned with her boyfriend. I let the police know that I believe that her use of the cellphone was the reason why she hit me from behind.

Another category of drivers you should be wary about on the road are the young Black and Hispanic drivers. Like the ladies,they are very aggressive and reckless on the road especially when they are driving in their domain areas. When you are in the far south and west sides of Chicago be very careful at the stop signs.

They normally do not stop at stop signs. They often drive through. They also often run red lights. You might think you have the green light in these areas, but to them you don't because while you have the green light they will still be driving across while you wait.

I had written in one of the earlier chapters about the dangerous driving behavior of the crazy cabbies. They are one of the dangerous and reckless drivers you should watch closely on the road while driving in downtown Chicago. Do not follow them closely especially in downtown because they make frequent stops and can stop without warning thereby making you to stop sharply. They can also cut you off sharply without any qualm of conscience any time they see a fare waiting in front of you. Whenever you see two crazy cabbies in a drag race on the street of downtown in pursuit of a fare in front, steer clear of them or you become a victim.

The CTA bus drivers are another category of dangerous drivers plying the Chicago roads. In the case of the CTA bus drivers,,it is not only that they do not always obey rules and regulations of the road like stopping at stop signs and red lights, they act like bullies of the road. They dangerously swing in and out of lanes with no consideration for the smaller cars. The drivers take undue advantage of the great size of the bus they drive to bully other drivers. And for the fact that they work for the government and also because the police tend to give them special treatment, the drivers do flout the rules and regulations of the road. If you are driving in the downtown area and you happen to find yourself driving beside a CTA bus, first of all watch the driver closely.

Then do not drive along the middle of the bus or it's tail area. The safest place to be is either in front of the bus or behind it. At these two positions you can never be affected by whatever the driver does.

If you are a regular driver on the roads and you have not had an encounter with the dump truck drivers, you must be very fortunate. Personally I have had my windshield cracked two times as a result of the careless driving behavior of the dump truck drivers.

I personally think the dump truck drivers should receive a special attention from the police. Many times they drive on the highways and expressways with uncovered loads of either rocks or pebbles which land on the windshield of unsuspecting drivers who drive behind these dump trucks.

Dump truck drivers don't seem to obey any speed limit. They rarely yield to smaller cars wherever the rules require it They act like bullies on the road as they cut off smaller cars with impunity almost daring the smaller car drivers to get off their way or get hit.

Chapter 13

CAB SERVICE THIEVES

There are a few miscreants among the cab riding public who love the services of the cabbies but want to receive them fraudulently without the least desire to pay for them They will flag down cabs like normal cab riders and announce a destination that sometimes is not their true destination, but an address where they can get away easily without the possibility of identification by witnesses. They use downtown as their starting base and then once they are in the cab they say that they are either going to the far South or West sides which are where most of such cab rides end up.

The perpetrators of this evil are mostly young people. Sometimes grown adults are involved and they operate singly or in groups. There is no art to know when you have a service thief in your cab. But when you pick a fare in the evening and he is trying to hide his face from full view or he is tentative with his destination, then be wary and alert. When the cab arrives at the purported destination, they use various tactics to get away.

I have been a victim of service theft many times that I have lost count. Sometimes their tactics provoke hilarious moment for me as I watch them get away without paying. I had driven cab for only about three months when I had my first encounter with a service thief. He was a male hispanic about 35 years old. He was well dressed and there was no way you could think such well dressed individual could be into this.

I picked him up in downtown and he was going to Western and Cermak. On our way, he picked up conversation with me. He began by asking about my welfare and the cab business. He spoke very intelligently and articulately. He pleaded with me to stop at the gas station on Cermak and Ashland so that he could buy some snacks. He even offered to get me some coke if I so desired. I thanked him,but declined.

We arrived at the gas station and I parked in front of the store while he went in. Before he left he asked if I would want him to get me something to eat. I declined again. Of course I left my meter running. So after I had waited for him for about 5 minutes I became slightly anxious, but did nothing. I waited for another 3 minutes and he was not out.

I decided to check out if there were many customers in the store that might have delayed his coming out. To my surprise there were no queue of customers and my passenger was not in the store. I asked the store man if there was any man in the restroom. He checked for the keys and found them hanging where they were usually kept for customers to pick up if they want to use the restroom. I asked the store man again if remembered seeing a man------ I tried a description of him ------who came in to buy some snacks. He said that a man matching that description came in and bought a bottle of coke and left through the back door. I went back outside to my cab to see if he had returned. There was no trace of him even after I had searched around. He is gone. I looked at the meter and it was about $15 that has just been stolen from me.

As I said earlier, there is usually no known art of knowing who a service thief is.

It is after you have been robbed that you can know.

On this beautiful spring night at the busy Navy Pier I picked up 3 black teenage boys all wearing hoods over their heads even though it was not all that cold. One of them said they were going to Armitage and Kedzie in the Logan Square neighborhood area. Another changed the address after they had mutely consulted together. I could not see their faces because of the night and also because of the hoods they had on. I became suspicious and was really on the alert. My suspicion was heightened after we reached Armitage and Western and they once again changed the destination. My suspicion made me to ask them who was going to pay for this ride and one of them assured me that they had money to pay.

After about 5 blocks into Armitage from Western they asked me to make a right turn into a one way street and as we moved in, the street was becoming darker and there were cars parked on both sides of the street which made it narrower. I approached a stop sign and stopped. Suddenly the rear doors swung open and the 3 boys jumped out and fled to different directions. I just stood there for a while and was angry with myself that I saw this coming, but could not stop it. That is $18 dollars stolen.

Even though my cab services had been stolen several times, the emotional trauma of being robbed at gun point or harmed in the process, is far worse than some miscreants running away after being given a ride. At least I can endure this.

So to me, I have become more discerning whenever I pick up passengers by just assessing their looks to know if they are possible service thieves. But there was nothing that could give this young black couple I picked on Michigan Avenue, away as a possible service thieves. So when they announced they were going to Hyde Park, I did not get overly concerned because they did not look like the stereo type. They looked responsible and were in their twenties and looked like they were on a date.

We took the Lake Shore Drive and exited on 57th street. The address was a high rise apartment. As we got close to the address the young man informed me that on arrival to the address he would have to go up his room to get my money. I said no problem as long as one person remained in the cab.

So on arrival to the address, the young man disappeared through the dimly lit high rise apartment's entrance to go get the money to pay me. After about five minutes there was no sign of him, I asked his girl to call him. She said she could not because he took the phone along. Another five more minutes, the girl got up and said she was going to help him find the money because she thought he might be having problem finding the money. I protested and asked her to leave something behind in my cab for security. She did not have anything on her to leave behind. Off she went and disappeared into the apartment too. I waited for what seemed like fifteen minutes and nobody returned to pay me. I took a look at the meter and it was about 27 dollars. I did not know how to look for help since I can't even give a reasonable description of this young couple.

I looked foolish standing there waiting. I was really angry that I had once again been cheaply robbed. My consolation this night however, was that as I was about to drive away, another couple called out to me from the same building to take them to downtown.

This helped me to quickly forget what had just happened.

Generally speaking, cabbies are not overly suspicious or scared when they pick up white kids even in the nights because they do not fit the profile of service thieves. So on this very night I picked a group of four white teenagers at Grant Park and they were going to the Bridgeport neighborhood.

It was a new year eve night. I had worked all day and was getting ready to go home so that I could attend the new year eve church service to ring in the new year. I usually close work around 10 pm even though new year eve night is usually a busy night till the new year arrives. Cabbies who work till the new year and beyond often tell of some unpleasant experiences with drunk passengers. I really did not want to be involved with that. That was one of the reasons why I close before the new year arrives.

I had all the boys sit at the back seat, having refused the request of one of them to seat in the front seat because it is my safety policy not to have a passenger sit with me in the front seat if I am going to a destination outside downtown in the night or to a dangerous neighborhood.

We took the Dan Ryan expressway and exited at 31st street and headed west.

We had just passed Halsted and headed to Morgan street. They instructed me to turn left on Morgan. After 4 blocks, they asked me to pull over. The street was lonely and dimly lit. I did not even make a complete stop when the rear doors swung open and the four boys jumped out and fled to different directions. I yelled out:"Help! Help!! Help!!! While still seated in my cab. Nobody came out of their homes in response to my cry. I could not but see the similarity in operation and execution of this robbery with that of the black boys. They probably went to the same "school."

Initially I was really mad, but I encouraged myself by the fact I had had a very good day making money and that I was already getting ready to go home for the day when I picked them and so it was no big deal if I lost 12 dollars which was what the meter read.

It is not usually my desire to work beyond 12 mid night. I close work on weekdays at 8 pm and 1130 pm on weekends. But on this day I had already dropped my last fare at the front of the University Club on Monroe and Michigan and was about to drive off and go home when the door man stopped me as a white man dressed in a black tuxedo with a black bow tie, perhaps in his forties followed closely behind him to enter my cab. I told him no because I had just closed. He pleaded with me to pick him and promised to give me a twenty dollars tip.. There were few cabs available at this time. I said no again and he persisted. Then I asked where he was going and he said Maywood. I thought it would not hurt if I make an extra 40—50 bucks before I go.

On our way he informed me that he would give me twenty dollars in cash and pay the rest with credit card.. That was okay with me.. We exited at Manhiem Road and headed to a strip club on North Ave. When I pulled into the compound of the strip club, it was almost 1:a m. He brought out his wallet and gave me a credit card. I demanded the twenty dollars cash as he promised, but he said that he thought he had enough cash.. He was sorry that he had to pay the entire fare with credit. I accepted. I did the calculation including the city limit extra and the twenty dollars and everything amounted to 55 dollars. I swiped the card and it was declined. I told him that his credit card was declined and he gave me another, This was also declined. H e gave another and this time it said the card was a fake credit card. I did not have to report that to him because he was in the cab watching. Finally he gave me the fourth credit card and it was declined also.

I suggested he try the ATM. As he moved towards the location of the ATM which was out of view from where I was parked, I jumped out of my cab to follow him behind just to make sure he did not disappear because by this time I had become suspicious of him.

He tried the ATM and could cash no money.

By this time I had begun to regret that I agreed to pick this man for this ride.. I should have insisted that I had closed and gone home. But the temptation to make extra bucks lured me into this. Anyway, the trigger had been pulled so I must have to live with the consequence.

"Man," I asked him, "how are you going to pay me?" "all your credit cards are duds and you said you don't have any cash."

"Would you accept check?"

"Yes, I can accept a check"

Then he began fumbling with his coat's pockets. "Oh, I thought I had my check book," he admitted.

"How are you going to pay me,,man?" I asked again.

He began talking on his phone. By this time I had already concluded that this man was a fake. I had already memorized his first name from the credit card. A thought came to me: why not agree to let him send a check for the amount by mail to me instead of wasting my time waiting for the impossible to happen.

So I called him and said to him, "I am willing to accept a check payment made in my name and mailed to Yellow Cab Company's address within a week."

He accepted to do that. I wrote my name,cab number and Yellow Cab Company's address and gave to him. I also demanded to have his name. The name he gave me which he claimed was his first name did not match the one I had memorized from the credit card.

"This is not the name you have on your credit card,is it?"I asked.

"No, it is not; the name I gave you is the one I am popularly known by."

"Please let me have the name on your credit card, if you don't mind"

He obliged.

I also demanded his phone number which he gave me. I had to verify the number by calling his phone. I called the number and his phone did not ring. He claimed that I did not write down the number correctly. He gave it again and I discovered that one number in the middle was the difference between the first number and the second. I called his phone again and this time it rang. I was convinced that he did that deliberately because he never thought that I would be smart enough to think of verifying the number. Having done all these, I drove off and headed home at about 1:45 am------the latest I have ever stayed at work since I began driving.

I am sure you would like to know if he actually sent the check to me. This is what happened. Three days after this encounter, I gave him a call and asked him if he had sent the check and he said he had not had time to do it. I appealed to him to try and send it soon and he pledged to do so. The next time I called, he picked the phone and asked with a harsh voice: "Who is this?"

"It's me,,your cab driver"

"Yes, what can I do for you?"

"I want to know if you have sent the check for 55 dollars to me?"

"What check?"

"The payment for the cab ride I gave you from downtown to Maywood last Saturday night."

" I don't know what you're talking about." and he hung up.

I dialed his number again, but he never took my calls.

After many attempts to call him failed I decided to give a break. I did not know what to do to collect my money.

I certainly thought about going to the Police, but thought the police don't often get involved with debt collection involving cabbies and service thieves when the alleged thief is not physically present and there is no evidence to prove the claim by the cabbie.

Of what use is it to go to the police to report that a passenger has just run off without paying and you can't even give a good description of the culprit. or his where about. So the ideal thing to do is to regard cab service thieves as one of the hazards of the profession and move on.

I did not quite give up on my 55 dollars. So I decided to call this man after about one month, to give him definite instruction about what he should do with my money. As usual, he did not pick my call. I waited until the phone went into voice mail mode"

"Hey Uzy,,I am the cab driver you are owing 55 dollars for the ride I gave you about a month ago. I am now convinced that you're a bad man who has decided to repay the good that I did to you with evil. That 55 dollars is my money and this is what I want you to do with it. Write a check for that amount and send it to the Salvation Army or any church close to you, in my name. Be warned that if you fail to do this and decide to "eat" this money you may receive some unpleasant consequences that could cost you more than 55 dollars. This is because I have transferred this case to the Divine Court of Justice for a righteous adjudication.

Chapter 14

TIPS FOR STRESSLESS AND SAFE DRIVING ON OUR ROADS

It is often said that obtaining a driver's license to drive on the road is a privilege and not a right. But to make the road safe for all is a mandate to every road user. So it takes the collective effort and responsibility of all road users to maintain safety on the roads. It takes just one irresponsible and reckless driver to cause a mayhem on the road that is capable of suddenly snatching away the lives of innocent road users in an accident that is avoidable.

Most of the accidents on our roads are caused by human failures and errors. If we would be a little more careful each time we drive into any road and realize that our lives and the lives of other road users may depend on how sane and careful we drive, driving on our roads would be a lot safer and fun. Many times some very careful drivers are lured into accidents by the recklessness of the "other driver" The "other driver", I was taught early as a young driver, was to be regarded for the purpose of road safety, as unstable and a mentally deranged man on the wheels. So for the decades I have been a driver on the roads I have always regarded the other driver as a possible madman on the wheels. Sure enough I have seen and encountered such drivers on the road and some of them were as crazy as advertized.

So when you realize that the "other driver" is possibly mad, it would be unreasonable for you to attempt claiming your right on the road from him. And because you not crazy as he is, you would yield to him even when he is flagrantly trying to cut you off. I am sure you would not mind also to move out of his way and if possible driving over to the curb, when you see him heading towards you in your own lane in his attempt to pass the other car in front of him.

It really takes a combination of providence, self disciplined driving habits,strict obedience to the rules and regulations of the roads and of course prompt obedience to the prompting of the sixth sense to stay alive on the roads. I can testify that I have been saved from many an accident, some of which could have been fatal, by just obeying my intuition or road instinct. To survive on the road you owe yourself a duty to obey your sixth sense. Your life could depend on it.

The main purpose of this chapter is to give you some useful tips from my over 17 years driving experience as a Chicago cabbie, from one of the world's busiest traffics, on how to stay alive and stress-free on the road. The only attractive resume I can boast about is my clean driving record. I drove cab for over 17 years in Chicago and retired without ever hitting any vehicle, pedestrian or cyclist.

1. TAKE GOOD CARE OF YOUR VEHICLE

Never you leave home with unsafe vehicle or a vehicle needing serious and urgent repair. If you do,,she might disappoint you and might even get you stranded on the road.

Listen to her attentively when she is complaining to you through various sounds and noises. It might cost you unnecessary extensive repairs if you ignore her early warning noises and sounds.

2. BE ALERT ALWAYS.

Driving distracted is one of the worst mistakes a driver can make. You know you can afford to read a novel while walking on the street or even take your eyes completely off the road for a while and still not collide with another pedestrian. Even if a collision occurs it might not be serious. But that's not the same with a moving vehicle, with all the horse power behind it, moving at a higher velocity with evasive reaction time very minimal.

That is why a driver must always be alert while on the road. Don't allow the use of modern electronic devices distract your driving. A split second distraction on a busy traffic could put a road user's live at risk.

3 DRIVE DEFENSIVELY.

Defensive driving is more often said than done. I have seen two drivers literally struggling to claim their rights on the road and it eventually led to their damaging their cars by side swiping each other. These two drivers were both driving in front of me as the left lane was merging into the center lane. The driver on the left lane started forcing his way into the lane of the second driver in the center lane.

But the second driver in the center lane did not want the driver from the left lane to cut him off. So he stuck to his guns even as the driver in the left lane persisted. As I watched them, I was thinking that this traffic hostility could end with no accident if each driver would elect to yield to the other. And none was willing and the accident occurred.

I have often advised fellow drivers that for the sake of their convenience and peace of mind that they should surrender whatever rights they have on the road to the " other driver, so as to maintain their sanity and peace of mind. Imagine what happens when an accident occurs on the road and you are involved. Whether you are the one at fault or not, you will be inconvenienced and every plan of the day will be affected adversely. It pays on the long and short runs to be a defensive driver.

4. TAKE NO OFFENSE ON THE ROAD

For your own interest refuse the temptation to take offense against the other driver no matter what he has done to you short of hitting your own car. Taking offense by yelling curses or obscenities at the erring driver will produce no benefit. Instead it could escalate into a full blown road rage and you are aware that people have suffered bodily harm or killed in road rages. So if the other driver acts irresponsibly, ignore him and yield to him. It would not hurt. Determine in yourself that you will never lose your cool to any recalcitrant driver on the road. It is not worth it.

5 LISTEN TO SOOTHING MUSIC

Driving always on a busy traffic like Chicago roads is a very stressful job.

I used music to smooth my nerves and keep me stress-free. If you are a music lover, you should keep a collection of music C.Ds in your car or have your radio dial tuned to your favorite music stations and listen to them while driving. For me, I love the gospel and the contemporary Christian music. Some time I change the dial to smooth jazz station.

Music has been an invaluable asset to me as a driver. When I listen to Christian and gospel music while on duty, their lyrics minister some calmness to me and help me get relief from the stress that accompanies driving for hours non stop. When you drive stressed, you are likely to be easily irritated,combative and aggressive.

6   BE READY TO APOLOGIZE WHEN YOU ERR.

In the course of my driving career, I have made many dummy mistakes on the road. But one thing I love to do immediately after I had offended the "other driver" is to apologize promptly. And that had on many occasions defused the anger of the "other driver" and worked to prevent any escalation of offense. From experience, quick apology is always accepted by nearly all drivers when an erring driver accepts responsibility for his driving mistake and apologizes to the affected driver. For example, I have on many occasions cut some drivers off in order to drop off fares at the curb side of the road. And usually I was ready to apologize with a smile on my face and a thumb up sign.

7.   OBEY ALL TRAFFIC RULES AND REGULATIONS

Traffic rules and regulations are made to protect road users from lawlessness on the road

Every road user is under mandate to obey these rules and regulations for safe use of the road by all. Many fatal accidents have occurred when drivers disregard the stop signs and stop lights. Nothing can be as flagrant as willfully running a red light or a stop sign on a busy intersection. Below are some practical tips for the road.

(a) Always give the vehicle in front of you a safe distance so that you can have time to react if the driver in front of you stops suddenly or gets involved in an accident. The reason why there are often multiple car crashes on our express and highways is basically because of the lack of the required safe driving distance between cars.

(b) Always honk before you pass a car to alert the other driver of your intention. Doing this could save an accident.

(c) Always make sure you use your rear-view mirrors to know what is happening behind and beside you as you drive along especially if you want to change lanes or make a turn. Take note that your rear view mirrors do not always see your "blind side"; you need to look with your eyes.

(d) "SPEED KILLS"------This is a popular slogan on road safety. Pay attention to this warning!

8   DON'T DRIVE SLEEPY.

Driving while sleepy is as dangerous as driving under the influence of alcohol.

Do everything within your power to get adequate sleep if you are going to drive for long hours. Or drink whatever your body accepts that can drive off sleep from you.

Some drink coffee or energy drink; others just take a bottle of coke and they are ready to go. For me, I always made sure I sleep for at least 6 hours every night. If for any reason

I was unable to sleep for 6 hours before my usual wake up time, I remained in bed till the quota was achieved even if it means that I would go to work much late.

I have discovered from experience that driving in a slow traffic, the type we often have on most Chicago express and highways during rush hour periods, lures a driver to sleep. So, as they say,wind down your window even though in a slow traffic that does not help much. A quick nap has always been the best cure.

9.   USE OF ELECTRONIC DEVICES

Cut down or if possible eliminate the use of electronic devices especially the phone while driving. The Chicago Cab Ordinances forbid cabbies from the use of hand held phones when on the roads with passengers. Use of phone while driving can be very distracting, even if you have both hands on the steering----that is you are using a bluetooth device. Driving while on the phone with a bluetooth device means that you have both hands on the steering while your mind and your thinking faculties are divided between your driving and your phone call. Safe driving demands your total attention on the road for the sake of road safety.

The driver with hand held phone commits one to the phone while one is used to manoeuvre the steering and this is more dangerous. Because not only is he driving with one hand, his mind and attention are also divided between the driving and whomever he is on the phone with.

I don't answer calls when I am driving. I also do terminate calls to anybody if I realize that the person is driving. I made this decision after I had heard a chilling story about a young man who was on the phone with his friend who was driving home from work. As they were talking, joking and laughing, suddenly he heard his friend scream and then followed by what sounded like a crashing vehicle and then a silence. That was the last time he heard his friend's voice.

10. ANTICIPATE THE OTHER DRIVER'S MOVES

One driving habit I was instinctively taught decades ago and which had helped me to stay alive on the road is the habit of anticipating the action of the other driver before he actually does it. When you are on the road, you need to be both reactive and proactive to the other driver's moves so as to avoid being involved in an accident.

It is not only with the other driver, but also with the pedestrians and cyclists. I can count about three times I could have fatally hit a dare devil cyclist and a careless pedestrian in downtown Chicago. But because I anticipated their moves, I proactively prepared myself to avoid hitting them.

.I count it as a huge blessing each day I went to work and had a safe driving day and returned to my house to sleep and work another day. Nobody should take this for granted because there are those who leave their homes for work each day but never make it back home, but ended in the morgue or the hospital. There are deaths always lurking on the roads seeking for the next victim. May that never be you.

Chapter 15

SOMETHING YOU NEED TO KNOW FOR YOUR NEXT CAB RIDE

It is difficult to understand why many Chicago cab riders are poorly informed about the basic rules and regulations for the operations of cabs, and cab drivers in the city. Even the information that spells out rights and responsibilities of the passengers concerning their use of cabs in Chicago are not known to them.

This information is provided in the TAXI RATE CARD or PLACARD, issued by Chicago Department of Business Affairs and Consumer Protection and usually affixed behind one of the front seats facing the passenger. Many regular Chicago cab riders have never read it even though they do see it often as they ride in cabs.

On the rate card is the information about the fares:

1. Flag Pull or Base Fare _____ $3.25

This is the amount at which the meter starts and the driver starts the meter immediately the passenger gives his destination address. As a passenger you should be observant to make sure the meter is not on before you have given your destination address.

2. Each Additional Mile _____ $1.80

This means that, for instance, you picked up a cab from State street by Randolph street and going to Halsted street, a distance of one mile. On a normal traffic the meter should read about $5.05 at the end of the trip.

3. Every 36 seconds of time elapsed -- $0.20

This is one aspect of the fare many passengers often query about. The meter is calibrated by time and distance. So if the cab is stuck in the traffic the fare will continue to increase at 20 cents per every 36 seconds of time elapsed.

4. First Additional passenger _____ $1.00

5. Each Additional, after the first passenger _____ $0.50

This means that for a party of 4 passengers, for instance, the starting meter amount would be $5.25

6. Vomit cleanup fee _____ $50.00

This rule was added in 2013. Even though this rule is welcome by cabbies, the city did not provide a guide on how drivers can collect this fee from the offenders who many times are drunk at the time of the incident.

7. Airport Departure/Arrival Tax ___$2.00

8. Seniors and Under 13 years:

Are not charged additional (they ride free)

9. Tolls are extra charge to the passenger

10. The fare does not include a tip

11. There is no extra charge for baggage/baggage handling

12. No extra charge for payment by credit/debit card

PASSENGERS ARE NOT REQUIRED TO:

1. Exit or enter the cab by the curbside.

The only exception from my own practical experience is when, it is not possible as a result of obstruction or a disabled in a wheelchair. Many good cabbies step out and stand by the door as the door opens and the passenger steps out safely. It is very important for safety reason for passengers to obey this important safety rule. I always as a routine, warned my passengers to step out by the curbside. I have seen accidents happen as cab passengers step out into oncoming traffic.

I recall one day on Michigan Avenue, during the afternoon rush hour, when one of my male passengers refused as it were, to obey my instruction to exit by the curbside. So when I saw him holding the door handle in readiness to open and exit into the traffic, I had already seen through my rear view mirror that a delivery truck was racing down towards us. As soon as he opened the door in readiness to step out and the truck was almost a second away from us, I shouted with all my might just as loud as a boot camp drill sergeant would: "close that door!"

He promptly did just as the truck whistled pass close to my cab. When he realized that he could have been hit by the truck had he ignored me, he looked penitent and said he was sorry. His friend who had already stepped out by the curb side and saw what nearly happened, commended me.

2. It is the responsibility of the passenger to tell the cabbie his destination address as specific as possible. During chauffeur license training cab drivers are taught to always repeat to the passenger the address he had given in order to confirm that the cabbie heard the passenger correctly. From my experience most passengers do not listen to the driver's repetition of what he thought he heard. The passenger gets furious when the driver takes him to an address he thought he

heard the passenger say. There are many streets in Chicago that sound alike. For example, Addison// Madison, Hermitage/Armitage, Fulton/Fullerton, Damen /Deming, just to name a few.

3. Every cab passenger may pay his fare by credit/ debit card. All city of Chicago cabs are now equipped with electronic machine to accept credit card payments. If the system is down as it does sometimes, cabbies are supposed to have the manual machine to process the payment.

4. The passenger has the right to ask his driver to stop the use of all mobile electronic devices while driving. If the driver fails to stop, the passenger could call 311 to report the driver.

5. It is now a class 3 felony offense punishable by up to 5 years in prison for a battery of an on duty cabbie. This law came to be after incessant physical attacks on cabbies by some unscrupulous members of the public. Taxi cab leaders lobbied hard for this law to be enacted and posted in all Chicago cabs.

SHARED RIDES

Shared ride is a cab riding plan available to passengers traveling to and from the airports to downtown. It is called shared rides because each passenger pays a flat rate when two or more passengers are picked up at one location and are going to different addresses within the shared rides zone in downtown.. Airports shared rides zones are: Fullerton avenue in the north, 22nd street (Cermak) in the south; Ashland Avenue in the west, and Lake Michigan in the east.

The shared rides fares are as follows:

O'Hare Airport To Downtown --- $24.00

Midway Airport To Downtown ---$18.00

O'Hare/Midway To Midway/O'Hare ---$37.00

TIPS FOR YOUR NEXT CAB RIDE

1. If you need a cab ride, stand at the curbside of the road and the moment you see a cab approaching, just raise your hand. You do not need to wave your hand, except if you think the cabbie did not see you

2. As the cab is approaching, observe the cab's dome light. If it is on, that means the cab is available for hire. But if it is off, that means the cab most probably has a fare.

3. When you enter the cab, most cabbies will greet you and try to be friendly with you. Try to reciprocate. You never know, a lively conversation can begin between you and your driver. When you are in the cab and you have given the driver your destination address, you don't need to inform the driver by what method you would be paying your fare, for example, by credit card.

Your cabbie is required to accept any method of payment approved by the city of Chicago. Some drivers, on being told before the trip starts that payment would be done by credit or debit card would claim that the system is down and so deny you the ride. Whereas at the end of the trip you whip out your credit or debit card to make your payment, at this point, he has no choice except of course, he refuses to accept the credit card and does not get paid.

4. Again, it is important that you be precise when giving the driver your destination address. The driver has been trained not to move until he knows exactly where you are going. As soon as the driver moves put on your seat belt and relax. Seat belt is very important especially when you are sitting at the back seat of a cab with protective shield in between you and the driver. Cabbies stop frequently and suddenly. The seat belt prevents the possibility of your hitting your face at the shield.

While you are on your way, be at alert and study your cabbie's driving behavior. If he is doing 40 MPH on a 25 MPH street, or he does not stop at stop signs or he runs the red light, I can tell you that your driver is a crazy cabbie. Give him a warning and if he reacts angrily, tell him to stop. You may now call 311 to report him. But you know, it is easier said than done. Most passengers would ignore this bad driving behavior and do nothing.

5. At the end of the trip, please step out by the curbside. It is really dangerous to step into the traffic side. After you have stepped out, stop for a moment before you close the door of the cab and take a look at the seat to make sure you are not leaving any of your belongings behind, for example, keys, cellphone, wallet,etc. You can't believe the kind of valuables cab rider forget in the cab.

If you forget a belonging in the cab, call the cab company or affiliation to report. Make sure you give the number of the cab and its color. Majority of times these items are recovered and deposited at the lost and found. Except in cases where incoming passengers see the item and take it without the knowledge of the driver.

6. Before you finally shut the door of the cab, take a mental note of the cab number, its color and company or affiliation just in case you forget something.

7. Finally, compliment your driver if his driving and general attitude was good. May your next cab ride bye pleasant and memorable.

INTRODUCTION

I'm Not a Crazy Cabbie, is a repudiation of the general characterization of Chicago cab drivers as the ill-mannered, uneducated dreg of the society and sometimes reckless and crazy drivers on the roads and streets of Chicago

When I left my home country, Nigeria, with my four young children to join my wife in the USA in 1994, I did not have the inkling that I would end up driving cab for a living. I had a master's degree in curriculum studies and had taught for eighteen years in the Nigerian federal educational system before coming here. My wife is a registered nurse had earlier come to the USA in 1990 after she was offered a contract by a Chicago based hospital to work here.

In spite of my dislike for taxi drivers and disdain for cab driving, I was forced to consider driving cab. The reasons being that my wife worked the night shift and as a result I was the saddled with greater responsibility of caring for our children. My children needed me most during the morning and afternoon school runs, when their mom would be sleeping.

Also after we had transferred our children to a private

Christian School, the fees began to put serious strains on the family finances which at that time depended solely on my wife's pay. So driving cab became the best alternative for me to be self employed as well as able to have time to care for my kids.

I trained and began driving cab in January, 1996 and loved it until I retired in June 2013 to answer another important call upon my life. I wrote this book to tell my story as a Chicago Cabbie. Also I have written this book to reveal who really Chicago cabbies are and the challenges they face in the performance of their job in Chicago. Chicago cab riding public deserves the right to know whom they daily entrust their lives to drive them to their destinations.

During those years as a cabbie in Chicago I had interacted with thousands of cab drivers in Chicago and had closely studied their behavior both off and on the roads. I can therefore report as an insider with a disinterested perspective that over 95% of Chicago Cabbies are good and responsible cabbies that the people of Chicago can trust.

This book also provides a lot of information about:

------The Crazy Cabbies and how to identify them.

------Why Chicago Cabbies, in spite of their numerical strength cannot have a united organization to fight for their rights, especially the highhanded rules and regulations and the poor response of the City leaders to the plights of the Cabbies in Chicago.

------How does a cabbie answer the call of nature when he is busy driving in the streets picking up and dropping off fares and there are no drive through restroom for Cabbies anywhere in downtown Chicago.

------Women of easy virtue who have made the Cabbies an easy target for their illicit desires.

------Some cab riders who have perfected the art of stealing cab services from cabbies.

------The odd and weird passengers.

------The Cat and Mouse relationship between the Cops and Cabbies.

------How to make your next cab ride a stress free ride.

------Finally you might want to know some of the practical and common sense driving behavior that helped me drive cab for over seventeen years in the crazy Chicago traffic without for once hitting any car, a pedestrian or even the dare devil messenger cyclist.